Nick Robinson's

Marketing Toolkit

Dedication

To my wife Janice.

I would also like to acknowledge the enormous
contribution made to this book by the 4000-plus
delegates to date who have attended my advertising
or PR workshops, and shared their experiences with
the Marketing Guild.

Nick Robinson's

Marketing Toolkit

MERCURY

First published in 1989 by Mercury Books
Paperback edition published 1991 by
Mercury Books
Gold Arrow Publications Ltd
862 Garratt Lane
London SW17 0NB

Set in Palatino by Phoenix Photosetting
Printed and bound in Great Britain by
Mackays of Chatham PLC, Chatham, Kent

British Library Cataloguing in Publication Data
Robinson, Nick
   Nick Robinson's Marketing Toolkit
   1. Great Britain. Marketing by small firms – Manuals
   I. Title
   658.8

   ISBN 1–85252–038–8

CONTENTS

Part. 2. MAKE YOUR DIRECT MARKETING MORE PROFITABLE

CONTENTS

Part. 3. STRATEGIES TO GAIN EXTRA BUSINESS

INTRODUCTION

The Power of Leverage

How to increase your sales by one third without increasing your promotional costs

Who first said, Give me a lever long enough and I will move the world? If you want to move your market, and gain more profit with less outlay, one way is to acquire a lever. This book offers many practical and proven ways to apply the power of leverage to your marketing. Let me illustrate this with a deliberately simplistic example.

Suppose you have £10,000 in your promotions budget. You'll probably agree, it should not be difficult in principle to cut it by 10 per cent, simply by trimming waste.

Next, you increase by 10 per cent the number of sales leads pulled in by your publicity. This is not too hard, if you follow the tips suggested in this book.

Having got the sales leads, you improve their

conversion-to-sale ratio by 10 per cent. Again, not impossible, if you work at qualifying your leads, and packing more power into sales literature and proposals as this book suggests.

You've just gained a 30 per cent increase in your return on budget without really trying! Let me demonstrate:

£10,000 × 10% saved = £1000. Put that £1000 back into the budget = £11,000.

If £10,000 gave you, say 1000 sales leads, £11,000 can be expected to give you 1100. But when you further increase the intake of leads by 10 per cent, you now get – not 1100 – but 1210 leads.

If your sales leads normally convert at 10 per cent, you will now get 121 orders. However, if you go on to improve your conversion to sale by just 10 per cent, you will gain 133 orders.

That is 33 more orders (33 per cent of 100), gained without increasing your budget. Just imagine, how much your *profit* will also gain, if you can increase your sales volume by one third in this way but without increasing your promotional costs!

True, the real world does not respond so readily to textbook examples. And if it was really as easy as that, all marketing directors would live in a chateau in France and write textbooks on how they did it.

But this book attempts to show you how, in step-by-step detail and using reasonable common sense, you *can* reliably improve your marketing results.

Not always by 33 per cent. Sometimes by just 5 per cent – or as much as 100 per cent! You can apply these ideas regardless of your type of market. They'll work for you whether your budget is virtually non-existent or – like some big consumer advertisers – is more easily weighed than counted. You can profitably apply these strategies if you run a marketing department or use an agency or do your own advertising and sales promotion.

All depend upon the principles of leverage: that is, reliably getting *more* for your effort (frequently by investing less effort). Let me show you what I mean . . .

How to choose the right promotional technique

If you're absolutely sure you know the difference between advertising, sales promotion and direct marketing, and when to use each, please don't skip this chapter. Because you're wrong.

'Which promotional method should I use? Would I be better off placing an ad in my local or business journal? Or mounting a direct mail campaign? Or offering a sales incentive of some sort?'

These are questions my delegates have often asked, and of course the only accurate answer is 'it depends . . .'. Trouble is, if you give that answer on stage it sounds as shifty as the Lawyer's Gambit, and about as useful. (Does *your* lawyer also have that infuriating habit of saying 'On the one hand . . . But on the other . . .'?)

Instead, here are rule of thumb ways to judge what should be the most cost-effective promotional solution to your marketing objectives . . . plus some fast definitions of the terms used in this book.

Like epigrams, these illustrations have hopefully the strength – but also the weakness – of brevity.

First, how are you currently selling to your market? If you're marketing, say, industrial capital equipment (like a packaging machine) your sales process might resemble a tall pyramid.

At the bottom are unknown individuals who should be in the market for your product (but you don't know that yet). At the top are a very few individuals who are highly qualified, that is, they have shown they need your wares, have the budget to purchase them, and the authority to specify or order them.

In the middle is a progression of steps leading hopefully towards the sale.

To move your potential customer from the base of the pyramid to the top may take several months, many contacts and much expense, because you're selling a high-value product, requiring approval from several decision-makers.

You may also use many different promotional techniques at each stage. For example, at the top of the pyramid, your techniques will probably include *direct selling* to a qualified individual or group. Below that we have the *sales promotion* – the device that gets potential customers to respond to your offer, or at least, to respond faster than they normally would: 'if you can finalise the order by the end of this financial year, we'll authorise a 5 per cent discount'. (Yes, I know that 'sales promotion' is defined in other ways, in different markets.) Below this is the personal contact of *telemarketing*, perhaps to check if they really have the need or budget or authority to specify your wares.

Below this is the less personal, but still closely targeted,

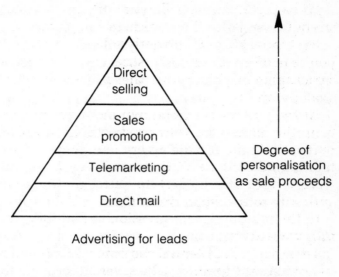

Figure 1   Typical multi-step model for industrial marketing

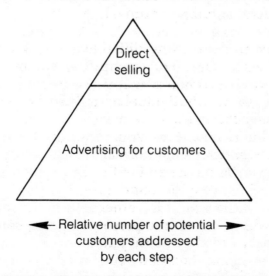

Figure 2   Typical two-step model for retail sales

approach of *direct mail*, probably to invite them to respond or clarify their needs in some way.

At the base, is the broad catch-all method of *advertising*, whether via print or product cards or loose inserts or tv or radio or posters . . . the vehicles are endless. An industrial firm may advertise simply to get sales enquirers, who are then laboriously progressed up the sales pyramid using different methods at each step.

That's one of the classic models of industrial marketing. But suppose instead you're selling plastic gnomes out of a garden centre. (One Marketing Guild delegate actually had this problem.) Your sales pyramid is a lot flatter, the selling period far shorter, fewer contacts are involved and the cost per sale is low. Of course, all that has to be, because the unit of sale is much smaller – just a few pounds. You may use advertising to get customers into your garden centre, and direct selling when they're there, and that's it.

So in answer to the question, *which method do I use*? the answer is deceptively simple. Do you know your potential customers, by name and location? Are they easily accessible? (Then perhaps direct mail or telemarketing or some other highly targeted, personalised approach will score.)

If you don't know them by name or can't reach them, you have to entice them to reveal themselves or to come to you. (Maybe advertising or sales promotion is the answer.)

This simplicity is deceptive, because in the real world you'll have a mix of customers or prospects, some more or less known to you, many unknown. Each will be at different steps on the sales pyramid. Your most profitable solution may demand a mix of techniques.

INTRODUCTION

For example, suppose you own a department store. Your January sales are coming up. So . . .

1. You run a big ad in the local newspaper and on commercial radio, revealing the bargains and inviting people to call in. That's *advertising*. It attracts all-comers.

2. You announce in your ad that you're celebrating your 50th anniversary and on Day One of the sale, everything in your window will be marked down to 1939 prices. A shirt for a shilling . . . a suit for five pounds. That's *sales promotion* because you give a temporary incentive to purchase.

3. Further, you tell the local press, tv and radio stations in advance about your amazing 'pre-war' promotion – so they can get their people in place to report the queues (and tussles) that will inevitably ensue. That's *public relations* (though some may call it 'publicity').

4. You also mail personal letters to your top credit account customers, revealing what they bought last time and telling them about the similar lines you now have on offer at fantastic savings. That's an astute use of *direct mail*.

5. You telephone your largest customers, to say the same thing and perhaps add a personal invitation to your exclusive After-Sale Cocktail Party. That's *telemarketing* (with a touch of public relations and sales promotion).

Suppose you do all these things. And you also insert leaflets about your sale into up-market magazines and newspapers delivered locally (by arrangement with your newsagent). And you drop handbills through letter-boxes in affluent neighbourhoods. And you sponsor college students throughout your sale to walk around town dressed as clowns and carrying sandwich boards. What do you call that?

I call it a lot of fun. (I believe that making money is the most fun that anyone can have, with their clothes on.) But technically, you might call it a *campaign*. It uses several techniques, and each is appropriate to customers at different steps on the sales pyramid. All the way from the person you've never met to the repeat, high-value customer who's become virtually a friend.

Does it really still matter what we call each technique? Besides, the stock definitions of advertising, sales promotion, direct marketing, whatever, are increasingly blurring into each other. I hope this book will demonstrate that.

A far better question to ask is, should you be using *any* promotional techniques in your company?

Delegates often ask it. To borrow the Lawyer's Gambit, the best answer is 'yes and no'. Let's take the case of one company I worked with. It designs highly specialised computer systems. They are used with commercial communication satellites (the ones that let you talk from Milton Keynes to New York, even more clearly than you can talk to Milton Keynes).

This company does *only* that. It's a strategic supplier, serving its industry worldwide. Suppose you're its marketing director and you want more sales . . .

Would you take prestige ads in the technical press and quality dailies, to advertise your capability? Or should you spend slightly less than the national debt, to rent poster space at Heathrow airport? How about hiring a stand for one week at Birmingham's National Exhibition

INTRODUCTION

Centre (it'll cost you only a little more than acquiring the lifetime freehold on a Birmingham office)?

Not for this purpose, you wouldn't. You have only a dozen or so (legitimate) customers in the entire world. Governments. Big firms. They already know you – in shocking detail – and more about you than you know yourself.

Would you use direct mail or telemarketing? *Whatever for?*

So what do you do? Simple. The company I have in mind hosts private technical workshops. That's all the formal promotion it does and it's all it needs. A dozen or so of its technical people regularly meet to brainstorm typical engineering problems with other technical staff from a customer or prospective customer. They exchange state of the art information, within the bounds of discretion and commercial confidence.

Hard sell is not necessary. Next time the customer needs specialised help it remembers that very discreet company which seemed so quietly knowledgeable at the workshop . . . and it calls them.

Is this sales promotion or public relations? Both. (Sales promotion is *anything* that advances the sale faster than it would normally proceed. And sometimes, the most profitable kind of 'public' relations is intensely private.) But if you asked this company, do you use advertising or sales promotion or direct marketing or public relations, they'd say No. And they'd be right.

Because such terms have become badly outdated. Conventionally, they tend to refer to *open marketing channels*. By these, I mean the public carrier routes of press or tv or radio advertising, the post or telephone, the editorial sections of the media . . .

Yet this is not the way many marketing-astute companies do their business today. The closer they know their current or potential customers, the less they need 'open marketing channels' and the easier it is to define their own channels, which are more effective, more credible, and more confidential. And the more controllable their marketing becomes.

Let me give you just a few examples of 'closed communication channels' taken from my own clients:

The *videoconference link*. This multi-national company hooks up its dealers in a private videoconference, nation to nation, to announce its annual range of new products.

The *e-mail bulletin*. A software firm introduces every new package and enhancement to its prime potential and current customers in seconds, and confidentially, via their electronic mailboxes. (It uses the British Telecom service Telecom Gold. Many other e-mail channels are now available.)

The *magalog*. This billion-dollar temporary staff company retains its 'temps' longer than all others. One reason among many is, it gives them its own top quality magazine. Not a new idea? In this case, it's a *very* new idea. Alongside the editorial are free samples, discounts and vouchers on up-market products which are only available to its temps. (Hence the term 'magalog' – a magazine plus catalogue.) Its staff perceive they get 'extra value' working for this company. They stay longer and recommend it to their friends.

The *hotline*. A financial services company records 'hot' market information on a two-minute tape, changed daily. Customers phone in to hear the recording. Only major customers gain this exclusive telephone number and every three months the number itself is changed for security reasons. Guess whom these customers regard as *the* most authoritative vendor, when buying financial products?

Are these techniques advertising, sales promotion, direct marketing or just good public relations? Who cares? The firms concerned certainly don't. Instead, these novel techniques illustrate the power of leverage.

You can apply it too. It's what the rest of this book is about.

PART 1

Pack more power into your advertising

1

HOW TO FIND THE TRUTH ABOUT A JOURNAL'S READERSHIP CLAIMS – AND SELECT THE BEST AD SCHEDULE

Have you noticed that every magazine or newspaper in any given category offers better value for money than any of its competitors? Or so say the brochures you get from their ad sales departments. And they are not allowed to lie, are they? For example, consider the claims made in media packs put out by the big engineering magazines:

Chartered Mechanical Engineering goes to readers' homes, has the endorsement of the Institute behind it, and is (it claims) the most regularly read engineering journal.

Machinery & Production Engineering is more frequent than any other, twice monthly, and it carries more advertising than the rest. That must prove something . . . satisfied advertisers, and all.

Design Engineering is targeted more precisely, it says. So your ad budget is better concentrated on the right people.

Eureka carries the highest-quality editorial, so its credibility and impact is that much greater.

Thank you, but *which do I choose?*

First, some suggestions on what not to choose – at least, without some investigation.

1. *Audited or merely publishers statement?*

Suspect deeply the claims of journals whose circulations are not verified by ABC (Audit Bureau of Circulations). And publishers' statements to the effect that they are printing 50,000 copies mean nothing: how many will reach their destination or, in the case of consumer journals, get sent back by the newsagent unsold? Likewise, distrust those which promise a bumper promotional boost to the next edition. Sure, more may flood into the market but will the market read it?

Just consider the case of magazine A with 30,000 circulation which charges £1000 for one page. You can easily calculate that the cost per reader is 3.3p. That looks good value compared with magazine B, which charges £1500 per page and has a circulation of 25,000. Its cost per reader is 6p.

And yet . . . how many copies of magazine A ever get opened? Even audited circulation figures mean nothing if one third of the journals are tossed away unread, possibly before even reaching their addressee (polythene wrappers scream 'junk mail' to many secretaries).

If only 20,000 of magazine A are read, the cost per reader is 5p.

It gets worse. Suppose that only 15 per cent of readers actually see your ad at all (that's not unusual according to ad readership surveys), you are reaching only 3000 readers. Cost per reader is now 33p.

Remember that only perhaps 20 per cent of readers

4

who see your ad will read beyond the headline: you are left with just 600 people who actually read your ad in any detail. Your true cost per reader is thus £1.67.

Are you happy with this? (For this price, you could mail about four direct mail packages, each containing far more response elements and information than a one-page ad – provided, of course, that you have the option of direct mail, which you may not.)

How does a £1.67 true cost per reader from magazine A stack up against the true cost from magazine B? If a higher proportion of readers open magazine B, and they read it in greater depth (perhaps because they respect its editorial quality), magazine B could show a much lower true cost per reader – despite the daunting figures on its rate card.

2. Paid subscription or freebie?
Ignore claims of superiority based on whether readers pay or don't pay for the journal. Research suggests there is little difference in readership of business journals between Controlled Circulation (free), Requested Circulation (free) and those Paid-for, in terms of advertising impact.

Why? A lot of people will request anything if it's free, so there's no special cachet about Requested Circulation. Nor do Paid-For journals command special respect – the subscription is probably paid for by the company anyway. Once delivered, all business journals compete for reader attention on their own merits.

Traditionally, it has been a different case with consumer publications, for which readers pay out of their own pockets. However, the success of free-circulation newspapers in attracting repeat (and presumably satisfied) advertisers suggests that even this traditional wisdom is now suspect.

3. *Cost per reader or cost per sale?*
Even true 'cost per thousand' is an unreliable guide. 'Cost per enquiry converted to sale' is the acid test – but it assumes that you are running direct response ads. This (inexplicably) may not always be the case!

So what's the solution?
In the absence of your own response data over a period (the only truly reliable guide), run your own Media Audit.
Print off some 1000 postcards. Send them to your customers – or prospect list – or at worst, a rented list or (failing even that) one compiled from directories which represent your market. At top, the postcard reads 'Magazine Readership Survey'. Then you list (or picture the front covers of) all the magazines you could relevantly advertise in.
Ask readers to tick (a) the magazines they receive, then (b) those they read 4 issues out of 5. Then they post it on to you (the postcard is business reply paid or Freepost.)
Ideally, you should conceal your business name as this will colour their answers. Use 'Media Research Unit' or a similar anonymous name, and your ad agency's address – at worst, your own home. (In this case, stick a postage stamp on the reply card.)
This idea works even if you offer readers no incentive to respond – but it works better if you do. For example: promise a modest gift or (retailers) a voucher to spend in your store. Better still, enclose a gift – a pencil. Not only does it lift response, but also your envelope will *always* get opened. Who can resist a crinkly package?

This survey technique can start a business relationship: you thank the respondent, reveal your identity, and put them on your mailing list. Only don't attempt to 'pay' for your survey by immediately bouncing back a hard-sell brochure or sending in the sales reps. (It's called 'sugging'.) Prospects will get very upset with you, and so will the Market Research Society!

Answers to such surveys will tell you more than any ad sales rep can, about which magazine is precisely right for your product or service. (And it may turn out to be one you never considered before.)

2

HOW TO WRITE A RESPONSIVE AD

While you may not wish to write your own ad, you will certainly need to brief a designer or copywriter, and check the agency's layouts and ideas. These steps will help you to distinguish those which are merely fun or beautiful, from those which should pull profitable sales leads. (The ideas that follow are extended in the Section on writing direct mail. Some repetition is inevitable, as ads and direct mail seek the same purpose: a response. The following is particularly relevant to ads.)

1. *Find the inherent drama in your product.*
This is the overwhelming single most important feature that distinguishes you and ideally is unique to you. (Or it is a benefit your competitors neglect.)

Interpret this as a benefit. For example, Signal was launched as not just another toothpaste, but a toothpaste . . . with a mouthwash in the stripes! Result – the consumer perceived added-value, and Signal became one of the 5 per cent of product launches which survived a test market. Yet a similar toothpaste, Stripe, was launched with the appeal 'You'll love the fresh taste in the stripes' and it flopped. Because no added-value was communicated. Does your main benefit sound interesting and plausible, when recited in the same tone of voice you would use to exclaim 'I've just won a million pounds!'? If so, you may have found what Alastair Crompton calls, in his excellent book *Do your own advertising*, your Drama. This was once called the Unique Selling Proposition (USP). It is now also mis-called The Competitive Advantage, by those who follow trends in management buzzwords.

The good news, for all of us seeking a Drama, is that this benefit does not necessarily have to be unique. Few companies really have an overwhelming product advantage. Instead, identify what's good about you, and concentrate on stating it Consistently, Aggressively and Persistently. That in itself may be more than your competitor – perhaps obsessed with flavour-of-the-month advertising – is presently doing.

2. *Picture in your mind your typical customer.*
What is his or her principal need from your product? What level of understanding do they have of it? What will best motivate them to buy? Phrase your key benefit in the shortest, simplest terms, as it applies to them. Describe (or picture) the customer enjoying the benefit.

Perhaps 'name' the customer in your headline: 'Design engineers – trim 40 per cent or more from your project times!' That's one way to stop all design engineers who glance at the page, while disqualifying the rest – whom you don't want anyway.

3. *Define what they have to do to get the benefit.*
Even the most intelligent reader is probably not at his or

her analytical best, when browsing through a journal. So tell them what action you expect now from them . . . Call your Hotline number for a no-obligation quote? Or complete the coupon? Or send their business card for a free Information Pack? Highlight this Call to Action in, for example, bold type or a panel.

4. *Summarise all the above in no more than 50 words.*
For example: Safegard is a disinfectant (a) strong enough to kill all household germs, yet gentle enough to use as an antiseptic on a baby's skin. (b) It is targeted at housewives with children, who will not necessarily believe this claim. (c) They should ask for it by name at chemists and supermarkets.

This strategy statement or template ignores a lot of interesting but peripheral information about Safegard, to concentrate the copywriter's mind. It is now much easier to evolve successful benefit-headlines, such as 'Trust Safegard . . . the one your pharmacist recommends . . . to do so much *more.'* And you can structure the ad to address this strategic theme.

(I am grateful to a delegate from ICI Saudi Arabia, who presented this case study – under a different product name – at a recent Guild advertising workshop.)

5. *Check that everything you say is 'on strategy.'*
Every ad, brochure, sales letter, poster or other piece of promotion which you produce about the product must follow that template, with necessary adjustments to reach different market sectors with different needs.

NOTE: The strategy statement is *not* an advertising slogan in itself (although it could be). It is the brief from which your creative people devise slogans – and all other copy.

11

NOW YOU CAN WRITE YOUR AD

1. *How many product benefits can you find?*
List them all. List the features too, and translate these into benefits. Steal good benefit ideas from your competitors, if they can also apply to you.

All products and services have at least six benefits. Sometimes the sixth needs digging for. It may be something everyone else's product has too (but is rarely mentioned). 'Our bottles are sterilised by live steam!' was the way one US beer firm advertised its beer. Every beer manufacturer does the same, but none had perceived (or mentioned) it before as a benefit. An extreme example, perhaps, but there is always *something* more you can offer . . .

A simple way to crystallise your offer in your mind is to write the coupon or reply card first. This should in any case be a mini-ad, summarising your entire sales proposition. From your viewpoint, it has to be the most important part: it brings you money.

2. *Prioritise those benefits*
Rank your benefits in order of their selling interest, to the reader. You might have 30 benefits. That's too many to pack into the headline or lead paragraph. You'll confuse people.

Instead, focus on the six biggest. Put the top one in your headline, and don't worry if it's a long headline. (Only posters need snappy headlines, because your readers are probably on the move. Long headlines – within reason – work for the captive reader.)

Use a second headline, too, to reinforce the benefit. Repeat the key benefit at least twice in different words or examples or proof stories throughout the body copy. Remind readers of it at the end or in the Post Script. List the other benefits in a panel or indented paragraph. Why not number them? Add a subhead: 'Here are 24 more big reasons you should order today . . .' Numbering benefits is a powerful device in itself, for stressing the value of your offer.

Remember that different benefits will appeal to different customers. Almost certainly, what your production or technical people perceive as benefits will not be mirrored by the market. And vice versa.

Focus Group research can be useful at this stage, in getting feedback from friendly customers on how *they* would rank the benefits of your new product. They might also suggest benefits which had never occurred to you.

Ask this group to tell you if they would buy your offer or not at a given price. (This yields you crude yes/no signals to the product's market chances.) But don't place too much faith in their replies to this last question, until you have actually tested the product and price in the market. What people *say* they will buy – and what they actually do – can be worlds apart!

A focus group is an assembly of some six–nine people on neutral ground, with a professional moderator who leads a discussion of two hours or so through a precise agenda of questions. It is recorded, with the group's knowledge, for later analysis. Usually, the group are not told the name of the sponsoring client until later, lest it prejudice their replies. Each is rewarded with a small gift for their time.

A series of carefully chosen focus groups which feature your industry's opinion-formers can themselves launch a product successfully, solely by subsequent word of mouth. But this departs from the arena of pure research!

3. *Write a letter to your favourite customer.*
In it you spell out clearly in a friendly way the benefits of your product. Put everything in, that could conceivably be construed as a benefit.

Follow the descending order of priority in the benefits – but summarise your most important reason to buy in a postscript.

4. *Now you can write your headline.*
Your headline is 80 per cent of the battle in an ad or direct mail letter. That's where readers start. Only 20 per cent will read on. So don't clutter up that valuable space with your company name and address – the weakest part of your offer. Put that at the logical place, the end. Along with your final incentive to respond: 'Call our special Hotline number now . . .'

Headline writers can learn a lot from magazine editors, particularly editors of *Readers Digest*. Any magazine that can get 16 million people to read it regularly must be doing something right. Consider how these cliché beginnings can add power to your ad: HOW, WHERE, WHY, WHEN, WHAT . . .

Research by Dr Henry Durant shows that headlines offering direct benefits at once, outpulled on average by four to one indirect headlines. For example, 'Get rid of money worries for good' outpulled by 500 per cent 'Leave money for your family after you're gone' (the latter promised a vague benefit at an indeterminable future – and introduced that ultimate anti-benefit, death).

'Now every home can afford summer cooling' out-pulled by 300 per cent. 'Don't swelter this summer.' The first offered a benefit, easily attainable right now; the second only hinted at a benefit.

Another doctor, Herbert H. Clark, a psychologist from Johns Hopkins University found that it takes the average person 48 per cent longer to understand a statement containing a negative than a statement expressing a positive. Moral: don't use negative headlines like 'You won't be sorry'. Try instead 'You'll be happy'.

Your headline should contain drama and urgency. It should ideally summarise the key benefit, and suggest that unless the reader immediately reads on, he will miss out on something interesting, valuable, or even vital to his life. The headline must make immediately clear what the proposition is.

Don't end your headline at the right margin, or the eye will stop there too. Break it into two or more lines, and let the first line of body copy start one third of the way into the page. The eye then progresses naturally from headline into copy.

6. *Cut your body copy by two-thirds – without losing a benefit.*

See what happens if you cut out the first paragraph – often this is just dead weight. Has your ad improved? Is the reader catapulted straight into the action? Probably . . .

Use 'bullets' – short, telegraphed statements. And take liberties with grammar if you must. Newspaper editors do, and they know what they're doing.

You now have the beginnings of an ad – or indeed a brochure or direct mail letter.

7. *When it's perfect, lock it away for three weeks.*
The gestation period for an effective ad is somewhere between that of the rat and the rabbit, about 28 days. In that time, it will develop extraordinary errors, inelegancies and superfluous statements – all by itself. Now wield your scalpel.

Editors know that every perfect piece of prose can be cut by at least 30 per cent without loss, and will gain greatly in strength thereby. (It's why they usually commission, say, 1500 words from their writers, knowing full well the page only has room for 1000.)

8. *Now improve it!*

3

HOW TO IMPROVE A PERFECT AD

There are three kinds of advertising: left-brain, right-brain, and no-brain. The latter need not concern us here. Advertising written to appeal to the left brain emphasises logic, because logic rules the left hemisphere – and a dull pinstriped personality it is. A lot of ads written to sell pensions are like that.

However, cigarettes, drinks and glamour cars are usually sold by ads written for the right brain. Because there's no logical reason to buy them, the right brain is all the copywriter has to appeal to.

Emotion rules the right side of the brain – *and that's where most buying decisions are (finally) made.* (The left brain then scrambles for good reasons to rationalise the decision that the right brain has already made.)

To generalise, the left brain is a stodgy adult, whereas the right brain is a playful egocentric child.

'Left brain/right brain' would be just another bit of discredited buzz talk, like the One-Minute Manager, the Boston Square, the Product Life Cycle and other escapees from the Guru School of Management. Except that it works. Our own repeated tests suggest that you do need to appeal to both sides of the customer's brain, to drive in response.

The left hemisphere says 'this offer looks reasonable to me'; the right hemisphere says 'I *want* it now'. Unfortunately, the client's decisions when choosing an ad approach (your decisions maybe?) tend to be made by the analytical left hemisphere, which is overly concerned with grown-up topics like budget and cash flow. And too often the ad reflects this.

Yet the most powerful ads blend Dionysus with Apollo, right with left brain. They appeal to emotional as well as rational needs, even when selling mainframe computers to dp managers. To seduce the right brain, your ads should:

1. Involve as many *emotional* reasons to purchase as you can. Among the most powerful are Fear, Greed, Guilt and Exclusivity. (This topic is also explored in the section on writing direct mail letters.)

2. *Illustrate the benefits* with word pictures. Photos and graphics help, but colourful descriptions can do the job nearly as well (for a serious prospect). And sometimes better, because you can invite readers to share an experience or imagine themselves enjoying the benefit:

    'Relax in your own personal swimming pool, as you watch the windsurfers skim across the warm blue waters of the bay . . .'. Work in the words 'imagine', 'picture', 'enjoy', 'discover', 'explore' . . . They involve the reader's right brain, the buying hemisphere.

3. *Introduce 'power words'* which are proven to sell products or services. Forgive my use of that schlock phrase 'power words'. But 'power' is itself . . . a power word. Other power words, to consider for any advertising you write, are:

free	yes
sale	benefits
exclusive	unique
offer closes . . .	secret
guarantee	discover
now	announcing
save	love
new	discover
results	proven
health	money-back
easy	money
suddenly	amazing
safety	enjoy
fast . . . and variations	on these

and, best of all,   *you.*

   To refuse to use these words, because they're clichés, is like refusing to travel in a car, because wheels have been with us for a long time.
   And don't believe that these words only work when advertising down-market wares to consumers, i.e. the man or woman in the street, whom many television advertisers still presume to be a gullible child. They work just as well (if laid on sensitively with a fine brush rather than a trowel) when advertising big-budget business goods to

senior business people. After all, a business person is just a consumer wearing a suit.

4. *Prune your ad* of dead words and phrases, by checking it against the following list. Does it contain (and if it does, cut them):

● desperate metaphors, 'fine writing', clichés, tired quotes from the late and great?

● unnecessary words ('In order to . . .' 'For the purpose of . . .')?

● pointlessly long words of three syllables or more (nonetheless . . . Comprehensive range . . .)?

● accidental slang or colloquialisms (it's . . . we'll . . .), unless this style is deliberately sustained for a purpose?

● the same words too often repeated, particularly at the start of sentences? (How often do you start a sentence with 'The'?)

● overly long sentences, or many sentences (or paragraphs) of the same length, or parentheses (i.e. clauses suspended in the middle of sentences, between dashes or commas, which impede the flow)?

● vague statements (such as 'most' when you can truthfully say '67 per cent')?

● passive verbs? (Turn them into active verbs.)

● latinate words? (Turn them into anglo-saxon. 'Approximately' = 'about'; 'manufactures' = 'makes'; 'modify' = 'change'.)

- hype? (Substantiate every claim or lose your credibility.)

- the future tense? ('You gain' is better than 'you will gain'. Imply the benefits are already theirs, the order is merely a formality that confirms them.)

5. *Have you avoided the temptation to be funny?* Awareness advertising can use humour, if it's really good humour. Cartoons have scored many triumphs. But jokes are a personal matter. If readers fail to see the joke, you've lost them, perhaps even offended them. If they do laugh, they're distracted: you have not seriously arrested their mind long enough to extract money from it.

   However, it's debatable whether Responsive ads should attempt humour at all. Unless you're a charity. A reader who reads your ad with a sympathetic smile is one who has identified with your problem. You make light of it, but they know it's no joking matter. They're prompted to help you . . .

6. *Does your copy bully, insult or intimidate the reader?* Is that rather obvious advice? Yet scan through any personal computer magazine (where many ads are personally designed by the advertiser's proprietor), and chances are that you'll find a lot of hectoring, almost abusive ads. If you criticise the reader's good sense, even by implication, you've lost the sale. Don't, for example, suggest he was crazy to throw money away by buying an IBM pc, when your pc does all that IBM can do and more.

   And don't tell him what he doesn't want to hear:

'You could die tomorrow. Have you made proper provisions for your family?'

Instead, compliment him on his wisdom in buying IBM (if you want to sell Brand X): 'You wanted the best. So you're the very person who will appreciate the *extra* benefits of Brand X. They help you go one better.'

And congratulate him on his foresightedness: 'I am writing to you because you have demonstrated that you care deeply and thoughtfully about a topic that is vital to us both, the need to safeguard our families.'

7. *Have you kept doubts out of the prospect's mind?*
If you say 'We're not too big to look after you,' readers will think 'They're too big'. Keep your copy positive, each word brimming with benefit. Write with a friendly smile on your face, the way a good sales rep will approach a prospect. It shows in your writing.

8. *Have you drawn on the Four Great Motivators?*
These are Fear, Greed, Guilt, Exclusivity (which comprise a modern quartet of Four Deadly Sins).

Exclusivity (or Vanity, in its working clothes) explains why publishers can sell directories of 'Who's Who in (name your profession)'. This is almost a licence to print money, because many people – celebrated or not – submit their names for free inclusion, then feel obliged to buy one or many copies for their friends!

Exclusivity was once called snob-appeal. It's visible in such appeals as 'Specified by the Tokyo

HOW TO IMPROVE A PERFECT AD

Olympic Committee', 'A personal message from the publisher', 'Your invitation to . . .'

In this century's affluent decade it's been repackaged as Prestige. Car manufacturers know well that men acquire glamorous cars like Mercedes and Porsches because these (apparently) represent mistresses. Witness the many ads which overtly identify a car with a woman!

Prestige also enabled the House of Campbell to raise over £17,000 for the Children In Need Appeal by selling a limited edition of just 600 bottles of The Edradour malt whisky – each bottle sold with a numbered Certificate signed by the Duke of Argyll. Snob appeal, of course.

Can you involve prestige in *your* appeal to the prospect's right brain?

Greed is an obvious motivator in many ads. It's the eye appeal of the luscious restaurant dish, or alluring beach, or gleaming new car.

But *Fear* is less often used well, perhaps because it can so easily misfire. (Prospects do not like being frightened.)

An innocuous way to use Fear is to list the people who have already responded to your ad. 'What advantage have they gained over me?' is the Fear trigger which moves response. These people can be neighbours of the household you're targeting – or the competitors of the company you are addressing.

A way to use *Guilt*, is to fix real postage stamps to the reply device. This is powerful with fund-raising appeals, because the prospect believes you cannot (really) afford them. It puts him under an obligation.

The 15 mistakes most often made in editorial PR

Do you make them? See inside . . .

This brochure effectively used a Guilt headline to draw delegates to a PR seminar

Readers Digest use Guilt when they include an actual 5p piece plus 14p-worth of postage stamps in their envelope (along with every other motivator under the sun, including a sweepstake offer, laser personalisation, 'rub off' reader involvement devices, money off vouchers, and lift letters, all in one hideously expensive – but obviously profitable – package). You know they can afford it. But . . . only a heart well hardened to such direct mail ploys could bear to pocket the money and the stamps, and toss that brilliantly engineered £1-plus sales machine in the bin!

An effective Guilt device in charity appeals (particularly when made among neighbours, or within professional or affinity groups, where members know each other) is to list all the other contributors to date, with a promise that your name will appear too (or be prominent by its absence).

The archetypal motivators, such as Fear, Greed, Guilt, Exclusivity, explain why the 'power' selling words work so well, although they are clichés. For example, the phrase 'buy one, get one free' outpulls by 40 per cent the same offer phrased '50 per cent off' or 'half price'. Why? That magic Greed word 'free'.

Likewise, the consumer society has conditioned us to expect instant gratification of our desires. So the Greed words 'easy', 'now', 'fast', 'enjoy it the very next day' are powerful.

Phrases like 'Don't risk . . .', 'Don't delay . . .', 'Tomorrow could be too late . . .'. 'You must respond by June 10th' appeal to Fear. Fear makes a good closing message, but a poor headline.

And 'you' summarises the motivator, Exclusivity: 'You have been personally selected by our Board of Advisors to receive this special offer', 'Only you can get this . . . if you act now'.

The Four Great Motivators were first propounded, I believe, by US scriptwriter Herschell Gordon Lewis. He became a millionaire with his films, Blood Feast, 2000 Maniacs and Colour Me Blood Red (possibly based on his experiences in US ad agencies). Despite that, I found him in conversation a charming and civilised man . . .

He then built a second fortune as a direct mail copywriter. Does he know something we don't? And should we learn it too?

9. *Have you created pressure to buy?*
Anticipate the procrastinator. Remind him what he'll lose by not responding now. (As a classified ad at the turn of the century said 'Send £1 and we'll get rid of your piles; or keep your £1 and keep your piles'.)

Put in 'cut offs' to urge action today. 'First 100 delegates gain this free autographed manual . . .', 'Offer must end Thursday . . .', 'Last chance . . .', 'To qualify for your special low Charter Member fee, you must apply by February 28th . . .' (But don't put cut offs in fund-raising appeals. You want the funds to *keep* coming in!)

Reward prompt action by offering a 'fremium' – or free premium item, a gift or bonus to those who respond within the cut off period. Yes, calculators still remain one of the most popular fremiums (you can't have too many, for your wallet, briefcase, drawer, home study, ad infinitum). Second best, to date, are travel and desk clocks.

Problem is, bribing the prospect now to close the sale can hurt you next time you want to sell. Customers will delay for their free gift. Or they'll know, if they wait long enough, you'll offer a bargain sale discount. And you also drive in a lot of freebie collectors, who have no intention of honouring your contract. (They don't know you, so even the nicest people will forgive themselves for blatantly exploiting or defrauding you.)

A better idea for business-to-business premiums, is the 'free information' pack or audio cassette. Make its topic precise enough to your product or service, and you deter those with little or no real interest – while giving a real incentive for those people really in the market, who need hard urgent facts a lot more than a free calculator.

10. *Have you repeatedly asked for the order?*
Sales reps call these 'trial closes'. Repeat them throughout: 'You will gain your free cassette just by mailing the reply card now.' 'We will mail your cassette within 24 hours so return the card now and enjoy your cassette without delay.'

11. *Have you made it easy to pay?*
Accept credit cards, even by telephone. Offer a free, no obligation trial or sample. In business-to-business marketing, don't ask for money up-front: you'll invoice them. (This sidesteps the problems business people often have, in extracting cheques from the accounts department.)

Don't wait for cheques to clear, before dispatching the goods – particularly if you've promised next-day delivery. If the cheque bounces on an order worth over £100, it is profitable to sue through the Small Claims Court. On small orders, your bad debt problem may have to be accepted as an overhead.

Accepting credit card payments (which must be authorised by the credit card company) avoids the risk of bad debt, and puts cash in your bank account quickly. But whether this benefit is eliminated by the 6 per cent or so fee per transaction plus the tortuous administration demanded by these firms, only you can decide.

12. *Finally check it all through again.*
Advertising veteran Shell Alpert has coined an acronym, PASSWORDS, which summarises a checklist of the factors you should have included – to add punch to your direct response ad.

P *Propose*: introduce the key benefits quickly. THE HEADLINE, PHOTO, SUBHEADS AND CAPTIONS.

A *Assert:* make those benefits appear dramatic and compelling. POWER WORDS.

S *Specify:* those benefits had better be precise, factual. NUMBER THEM.

S *Support:* give endorsements, testimonials, research data. CREDIBILITY FACTORS.

W *Weight:* name your satisfied customers, big name quotes and references. 3RD PARTY REFERENCE.

O *Overcome:* anticipate the sales objections, and throw them back in a positive way, as sales plusses. FREE TRIALS, DEMONSTRATIONS, SAMPLES.

R *Reiterate:* repeat your main benefits over and over, in different words. LONG COPY.

D *Dilemmatize:* show what the prospect will lose by delaying. And what (extra) benefits he gains by replying now. FACILITATORS and SWEETENERS.

S *Solicit:* ask for the order. And tell him how to place it. Make it easy for him to make up his mind and respond, by ticking a box, using a tollfree call or reply paid card. RESPONSE DEVICES.

Do all these things and your enhanced ad should sell and sell . . . provided, of course, that you're reaching the right people with something worth buying!

4

HOW EXTRA CREDIBILITY CAN MAKE
YOUR AD PULL HARDER

Proof statements are vital, if you want to outpull your competitors. Your market is sceptical at best. Why should they trust you? Their caution is understandable when so many watchdog investigations by the media have suggested that commerce can be a world of fraud and illusion. Quite unlike the media itself, of course!

To 'prove' your claims, should you hire a professional celebrity? Many will endorse you, for a fee. But many studies suggest that consumers will not necessarily believe their claims. The public will assume the endorser has been paid and probably does not use the product.

The once low-cost and squeaky-clean sports star is now the worst offender: in the US, sports stars can expect to earn three times their salary in endorsement fees.

Of course, such ads have been proven to have higher readership than others, because the celebrity attracts. But this can be a weakness, the celebrity becoming more celebrated than the product.

It's why Lorraine Chase was dropped from the Campari ads (or were they really ads for Luton airport?) and

"Unlike me, my Rolex never needs a rest."

Placido Domingo, possibly the greatest living tenor, has one over-riding ambition – to help more people, all over the world, understand and appreciate the music he loves.

To this end, Placido Domingo has learned 80 different operatic roles – an amazingly diverse and daunting repertoire, but also one which attracts the widest possible audience. He has also sung the lead role in 'My Fair Lady' and performed Zarzuela folk-songs, simply to interest more people in the power of music. In recent years his films, including 'La Traviata', have given pleasure to many who discovered opera first in the cinema. Very recently, Placido Domingo has completed the most

ambitious opera film ever made, where his Otello is directed by Franco Zeffirelli.

And now, Placido has added yet another career to his operas, films, videos and records both as a singer and a conductor. "My goal," he says, "is to be a real Music Director...to bring together the best conductors and best stage directors and the best possible casts."

So he has become Music Advisor to the Music Center Opera Association in Los Angeles, with the aim of building a new, world-class opera company. The range

of Placido Domingo's activities recalls the spirit of the Renaissance, where the most gifted craftsmen excelled in as many related skills as possible.

During 1986, Placido Domingo has used his remarkable voice as often as he dared to raise funds for Mexico following the earthquake in which so many people, including members of his own family, lost their lives.

To keep up with the ever-increasing demands on his time Placido Domingo, the Ambassador of Opera, relies on his Rolex. "This watch is perfect for me," he says, "because, unlike me, it never needs a rest. You could say it's one of my favourite instruments."

ROLEX
of Geneva

Endorsements from professional celebrities gain readers,
but do they sell product?

This brochure for the curiously-named PIG – a product that absorbs fluid leaks on industrial floors – pulls no punches in its use of customer testimonials.

Leonard Rossiter and Joan Collins were dropped from
the Cinzano ads (or were they Campari ads?). Instead,
try these ideas to make your claims credible:

1. *Testimonials convince.*
They should be from independent parties – satisfied
customers, professional institutions, the media, labora-
tories . . . If you have satisfied customers, ask for *their*
testimonial.

It's easier than you may think. Call fifty happy customers cold, ask them why they like doing business with
you. Ask them if they'd put what they just said in writing
– and authorise you to quote them. Perhaps as many as
half actually will. It's enough . . .

Publish their quotes as testimonials . . . preferably
with a photo of the customer. (You *must* quote their
name. A testimonial without a name is worse than
nothing. It suggests you have made it up.) Use these
testimonials in ads. In exhibition displays. In direct
selling. In retail-counter folders.

Even bind them together in fat books – one quote per
big A4 page. That way your testimonial file, when used
at the sales interview, looks impressive indeed.

An excellent business-to-business mailshot I once saw
was from a firm of conference organisers. It was an
autograph book, postcard size and one inch thick. On
further examination, it proved to be some fifty thick
vellum pages – a short quote on each from a happy client.
First page was a loose reply card; last page was the same,
but this time perforated and bound in. The cover read:
'See inside for 50 reasons we should talk.' The little book
spelled solid quality and reputation. Maybe it cost them
£5 each, to run off 100? But just one contract would

justify that, and I'll wager they got a lot better than 1 per cent response.

You can use testimonials even in local advertising. For example:

Suppose you have a small building firm. You run pictures of your delighted customers posing in front of the work you did. Run these as small ads, and repeat them regularly. Your customers become minor celebrities. They talk about you. (But be sure you get their permission in writing!)

Should you pay customers to 'advertise' you? It's a dangerous precedent. Consider barter instead – you'll do a small extra job for them free, or give them credit against their next order. A wedding photographer I know advertises his best photos continually to gain further business, and deflects questions of 'advertising fees' with a generous offer to pay the couple 15 per cent commission on future work that comes through their personal recommendation, i.e. from friends and workmates. In fact, he would be glad to give this commission to anyone bringing him work.

But . . . beware of the Reference Site Scam. It's tempting to offer people a special discount to install your product (usually a shower, or roofing, or double-glazing) because 'they are the first in the neighbourhood' and you want to mention them in your advertising. In fact, there's nothing wrong with this approach, properly run. But it's now been so discredited by cowboy operators, it draws media fire.

Give ample references to your 'proof statements'. Don't claim 'Research tests prove . . .', say 'Independent research by the Good Housekeeping Institute established that . . .' (Pedantry pays, when overcoming readers' suspicions. Be sure to stress the date, place and other detailed references to your 'independent tests' in a footnote.)

2. *Put a lot of your selling copy into the coupon.*
The reader identifies this as a non-selling space, so somehow it has more credibility. It also lets you repeat your main offer, so the prospect mentally notes: 'Yes, I agree to that' when he completes the coupon.

3. *Compare your product with alternative solutions.*
And give specific facts and figures. For example, the cost of renting a colour tv versus buying one; interest gained by your unit trust versus an ordinary building society account; the economy of a facsimile machine versus the cost (and inconvenience or delay) of postage, courier, or telex.

Credit your sources of information, particularly if they're official: it adds credibility. And officialdom cannot protest at your quoting facts which are in the public domain.

But beware of knocking a named competitor or product: it can backlash on you (see Playing David to Goliath, elsewhere in this book). Instead, ask: 'Does *your* supplier offer all this as standard?' Then list your features in terms of benefits. With a little thought, you may be surprised at how many you have.

This approach usually pays off in better response. First, it involves your reader in a quiz (*Readers Digest* addicts will testify to the appeal of quizzes, and quizzes are a sound technique in their own right, for adding impact to an ad). Second, it raises questions about the reader's existing source.

36

This technique can be particularly effective when you know the competition has an Achilles heel or two. My marketing consultancy used it to launch a contract cleaning firm. Cleaning is a murderously competitive business. Price rules, and our client was more expensive than anyone else.

Solution? We offered via direct mail and space ads a free booklet: '51 ways to get more value from your cleaning contractor'. (Not 50, but 51. Why? Using odd numbers adds credibility.) It comprised a checklist of places the customer should look, to tell if the cleaner was really doing the job. It detailed, in fact, the quality control audit which the cleaning firm's supervisors carried out routinely.

We asked the prospect to walk round his office or warehouse, booklet in hand. (Food processing plants, computer manufacturers and private medical clinics were especially responsive.) If he found more sloppy work than he liked, we'd give him a second opinion – and a free survey.

A gratifying number of prospects agreed they could not afford such poor quality work, and fired their existing contractors on the spot.

Involve the reader too, with a challenge: 'Spot the man who is *not* drinking Harp lager'. Or a puzzle: 'How many of these common mistakes do you make in English?' Or a totally inexplicable mystery: 'Why did these top travel agents choose Brighton for their own holiday?'

4. *Show before-and-after evidence.*
Diet plans do this, of course. But if your company in any way restores, beautifies, replenishes or improves a customer's life or business (and don't all successful com-

panies do this, in some way?) then *picture* the improvement.

Where the evidence is intangible, like a reduction in computer downtime, picture it as a bar chart or graph (preferably alongside a photo of the contented customer.)

5. *Sign your brochure or ad.*
Tuck in a small photo of yourself – or of your quality control inspector (this can be your production director in a white coat. If he's not ultimately responsible for quality, who is?). Alongside it, repeat in quotes your company's Pledge of Service:

'I promise you will enjoy this product, and gain value from it. If for any reason, at any time, our product fails to please, call your regional service centre. If they have not resolved the difficulty to your satisfaction within five working days, call me. I'll look into it personally. That's a promise. John Smithy, Managing Director.'

The end is a good place too, to put your product Guarantee, if you have one (you do, don't you?).

6. *Give a guarantee.*
Mail order firms have by law to give a refund if the product is returned within twenty-eight days. So make necessity into a virtue: give a no-quibble money-back guarantee. Fewer than 5 per cent will claim it, if yours is a quality product. If you're a retailer or dealer, or you sell through them, you probably operate some form of credit or replacement scheme but have you ever advertised it as a sales feature?

This is the Guarantee we have to live up to in order to satisfy you.

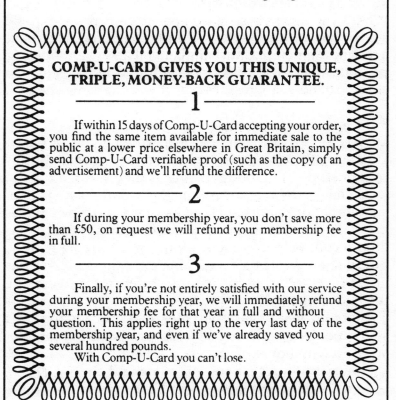

COMP-U-CARD GIVES YOU THIS UNIQUE, TRIPLE, MONEY-BACK GUARANTEE.

1

If within 15 days of Comp-U-Card accepting your order, you find the same item available for immediate sale to the public at a lower price elsewhere in Great Britain, simply send Comp-U-Card verifiable proof (such as the copy of an advertisement) and we'll refund the difference.

2

If during your membership year, you don't save more than £50, on request we will refund your membership fee in full.

3

Finally, if you're not entirely satisfied with our service during your membership year, we will immediately refund your membership fee for that year in full and without question. This applies right up to the very last day of the membership year, and even if we've already saved you several hundred pounds.

With Comp-U-Card you can't lose.

Guarantees work – and virtually any firm can guarantee its wares in some way.

I've heard clients say, 'everyone does that'. Maybe true, but does your customer know it? Probably not. Clients also say 'if we advertise it, everyone will exploit it'. Not necessarily true. And you may find a guarantee brings you more than enough extra business to compensate for the few cranks and frauds it will attract.

7. *Show a 'mission impossible'.*
What's the *worst* possible experience your product could survive? Set up the situation, and photograph it. If you have a real life example, so much the better. Parker Pen showed a pen which still wrote, after being found in the belly of a shark. So did A T Cross. Maybe it was the same shark.

8. *Cite third-party evidence.*
Do you have a newspaper article extolling you? A magazine editor's review of your product? Legally, they cannot stop you quoting it, even if they wanted to.

A well-known test case in the US involving Consumers Union confirmed that, as long as a reviewer takes prudent care in reviewing a product, a manufacturer has little recourse in the event of an unfavourable review. But in the event of a favourable one, the reviewer has little power to forbid the manufacturer from advertising the endorsement!

That information is apparently not known to the UK's self-appointed watchdogs: *Which?* or *What to Buy for Business?* So why not exploit a good review?

However, I suggest you play safe and check UK precedents with your solicitor – and in any case, avoid the ploy of printing quotes too selectively, as is sometimes done by desperate theatrical promoters. ('Utterly beyond belief . . .' *Evening Standard*.)

THIS MAN CAN GIVE YOUR COMPANY THE EDGE

It's amazing the number of businesses this man has turned his hand to.

Light engineering, vehicle repairs, plant hire, haulage, drainage, goldsmithing, dairy farming, high-quality woollens, private hospitals. You name it, he's made a success of it.

He's even made a major contribution to one of our best-known department stores, and if he sounds like some kind of superman we wouldn't disagree.

Because, in his way, he is.

The man with the amazing pedigree is none other than our senior engraver.

He's one of just a handful of craftsmen skilled in hand-engraving dies for relief-stamped business stationery.

He works for Eversheds, and he's helping to keep a time-honoured craft alive.

He works free-hand on mirror-polished steel, using a graving tool he fashions himself, to produce a quality of image un-surpassed by any other printing method.

The embossed gloss and lustre of Eversheds' hand-engraved stationery has lifted some famous names well above the ordinary, together with many less famous, but no less important for all that.

For all these companies the extra cost (though not as much as you might imagine) is well worth the extra edge in business terms.

If you feel your stationery presentation could be more distinctive, simply send your business card and current letterhead to our Business Development Manager, Robin Hales at the address below, alternatively 'phone him on 0727 54652.

Hand Engraved Stationery

EVERSHEDS
Since 1876

Alma Road, St. Albans, Hertfordshire, AL1 3AS

Better than a celebrity, picture yourself – or one of your key people – for credibility

41

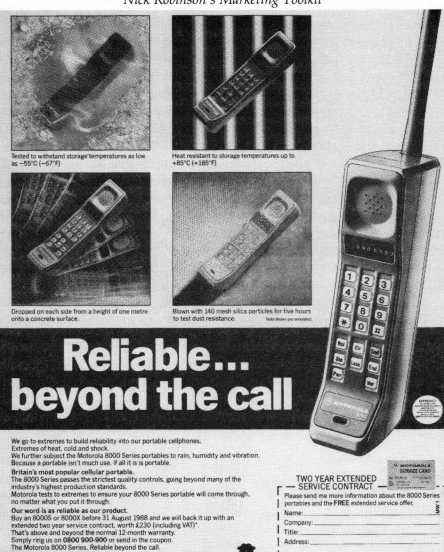

Tested to withstand storage temperatures as low as −55°C (−67°F)

Heat resistant to storage temperatures up to +85°C (+185°F)

Dropped on each side from a height of one metre onto a concrete surface.

Blown with 140 mesh silica particles for five hours to test dust resistance. Tests shown are simulated.

Reliable...
beyond the call

We go to extremes to build reliability into our portable cellphones.
Extremes of heat, cold and shock.
We further subject the Motorola 8000 Series portables to rain, humidity and vibration.
Because a portable isn't much use, if all it is is portable.

Britain's most popular cellular portable.
The 8000 Series passes the strictest quality controls, going beyond many of the industry's highest production standards.
Motorola tests to extremes to ensure your 8000 Series portable will come through, no matter what you put it through.

Our word is as reliable as our product.
Buy an 8000S or 8000X before 31 August 1988 and we will back it up with an extended two year service contract, worth £230 (including VAT)*.
That's above and beyond the normal 12-month warranty.
Simply ring us on **0800 900-900** or send in the coupon.
The Motorola 8000 Series. Reliable beyond the call.

MOTOROLA Cellphones

All tests are conducted under strict laboratory conditions.
For safety reasons, test reconstruction is not recommended.
This offer is available only on connections with MCS

TWO YEAR EXTENDED
— SERVICE CONTRACT —
Please send me more information about the 8000 Series portables and the **FREE** extended service offer.

Name:
Company:
Title:
Address:

Telephone:

To Motorola Communications Services Ltd., Freepost 4335, Bristol, BS1 3YX.

This 'mission impossible' ad for a mobile telephone adds credibility

9. *Offer a no-risk demonstration.*
But don't tamely offer prospects a trip round your factory
or display room (they know they can get that from your
competitors too). Instead, boldly promise 'Claim your
free seminar! An hour or a day packed with tips, ideas
and money-saving techniques . . . at a time *you* choose.'
After all, if you really give a good practical presentation,
that's what they'll get.

10. *Provide a free sample or trial.*
Truck manufacturers do this when they give prospects a
months') (or three months') trial. They know they can't
lose. If the prospect returns the truck, he gets billed for
rental. If he keeps it (and by the proven 'puppy dog'
principle of selling, he's now loathe to part with it), the
supplier gives him the rental period free.

Of course, freebie collectors will try to abuse your
offer. So if you're offering anything valuable, weed them
out by having them clip their business card to the reply
coupon and sign a statement that they are the company's
senior decision-maker for your type of product or service
and that they spend x amount or more each year on it.

Better still, 'rent' them your sample. Take their credit
card number, or their cheque. They get their money back
if the sample is returned in good condition. Air France
produced a 'travel brochure' on video cassette – which it
rents out.

11. *Be specific, specific, specific . . .*
Make your benefits exact. A great mistake is to attempt to
appeal to the widest possible audience, by means of a
general headline: 'Make more money now' is weak.
More powerful is 'How you can gain a 50 per cent return

Are you getting the best from your media budget?

15 important media questions vital to direct marketeers

1. Do you like the idea of paying 5% media commission (or even less) instead of the usual 15%?
2. Have you established the best size and page position for your advertisements?
3. Do you know the optimum frequency for each publication?
4. Would you like to extend your peak selling seasons?
5. Do you usually pay extra for premium positions?
6. Are you paying the lowest rates for your space?
7. Have you negotiated c.p.i. deals?
8. What can you learn from your competitor's media schedule?
9. Are you taking full advantage of short term opportunities?
10. How quickly can you weed out non-effective media?
11. What are you learning from A/B tests, regional tests, crossover tests, destruction tests?
12. Are you using the savings from short-term buying to test new media?
13. Are you aware of the new opportunities offered by inserts?
14. Have you seen how effectively television can be used in the direct marketing media mix?
15. Do you want media advice based upon unequalled experience of analysing consumer response?

Direct Response Media, the media independent that specialises in Direct Response Advertising. DRM is for clients who need better value from advertising but who are not necessarily looking for a full service. DRM have never failed to make substantial improvements in the performance of a new clients media budget. Direct Response Media Ltd.
Phone 01-940 2208 today – ask for Bob Holder, Judith Hatcher or John Goodwin.

DIRECT RESPONSE MEDIA LTD
Consultants in Direct Response Media
Quadrant House, The Quadrant, Richmond, Surrey TW9 1DJ.

Checklists help readers to qualify themselves, yielding many and more worthwhile responses in 12 months in penny shares with only £1000 invested.' Yes, you turn off all the readers who lack £1000 to invest, or who distrust the Stock Market. But they weren't going to buy from you anyway.

Quantify your benefits wherever possible. Numbers were once associated with magic. They still have persuasive power. Don't say 'whiter than white', say '10.7 per cent whiter than white'. Don't write 'Here are some of the many benefits you will gain', write 'You will enjoy these 11 benefits without delay'.

Incidentally, as I said before, *never* round your figures up or down. Forty nine is more persuasive than 50. And 51 is even better.

Little things count. Spell out why your offer is outstanding quality. Even if your manufacturing or quality control procedures may be nothing special in your industry, chances are the reader is not aware of the detailed care you take.

'Each of these figures is subtly different, because as many as six expert craft workers are involved at separate stages. They make it to order, just for you. No fewer than twenty-three separate pieces of pure white clay are shaped by hand, and carefully cemented together. These are then painted, again by hand. The figure is allowed to dry slowly in controlled humidity and temperature for seven days. It is then painstakingly lacquered with an impact-resistant varnish, etc . . .'

After all that, who can begrudge spending a few pounds more for it? (Even though *everyone* may make their ceramic figures this way!)

5

HOW TO USE 'KNOCKING COPY' ADS
TO DRIVE IN BUSINESS

When the market share dips, the first inclination of a tired copywriter on a mega-budget account is to attack the competition. In Germany, this is illegal; but in the US, it's almost obligatory.

Understandably so. The US has many more tired copywriters than the UK. Over there, Bayer slams Tylenol. Wendys Hamburgers slams McDonalds. And they persist, they persist . . . despite a famous *Readers Digest* survey which suggested that such 'knocking copy' ads actually promote the competition. People have short memories. The facts quickly dissolve, only the impression remains. And it may be the name of your competitor.

And yet . . . didn't Apple's Macintosh computer launch itself into orbit with a television ad, remembered to this day, which savagely attacked IBM? Doesn't every IBM-compatible personal computer now promote itself as faster, smaller, bigger-memoried or whatever than a pc from Old Blue?

'Knocking copy' ads *can* work, and harvest you a handsome crop of sales leads, but only if you observe these Three Golden Rules:

1. If you're David to Goliath, stand on Goliath's shoulders. If you really have a product or service benefit he lacks, attack him (within the bounds of law and prudence) for all you're worth. He probably won't care or notice. But the market will start to associate you with the market leader.

2. If both of you are Goliaths (and this can be true simply on a local or regional level), you could lose as much as you gain – if you mention the opposition.

3. If the competitor you want to attack is not a Goliath, where's the benefit in attacking him? Probably the market barely knows he exists. Why give him free advertising?

However . . . rules are made to be demolished. Two local advertisers could build each other into Goliaths, by covertly entering into a fun battle to increase market awareness of them both.

For example, two department stores once ran a pre-Christmas 'feud' on local press and radio, with pre-arranged themes that appeared to attack each other. 'Smithy has all these bargains . . .' 'But Jones has all this choice . . .'. It went on for weeks, drawing editorial mention and lots of readers (and customers).

Why go to all this trouble (and certainly drive a few customers to the competition)? Because, as every popular newspaper knows, conflict attracts readers. Interest in your feud will grow. People will even buy the paper just to see your latest ads. You may get editorial coverage for your 'battle to give the public the best possible deal.' (Of course, a journalist will understand what you are up to, and play the story tongue-in-cheek too – which is what you want.)

Finally, you could publicly settle the feud with a joint ad, picturing you both – to wish your customers a Merry Christmas. That's the way to double your business, for you *both*!

6

HOW TO PROMOTE A LOWER
QUALITY PRODUCT

Quality is *not* innate to any product. It is what the customer perceives. Andy Warhol once accepted multiple lecture engagements in different cities and sent along lookalikes to stand in for him. He reasoned they would perform just as well as him. The audience would perceive an experience of Andy Warhol, and be quite satisfied.

Is this fraud? Legally, yes, if customers pay and are deceived as to the nature of their purchase, regardless of whether they are happy with it.

1.   But sometimes, you can change the customers' perceptions in legal and ethical ways, so that they are more than happy with your product, even if it's not what they first imagined. And without deceiving a customer.

An apple grower in Vermont had a disastrous Autumn. Hail pitted all his apples. So he publicised the imperfections – as proof that the apples had been exposed to chill weather and (as everyone knows) this improves eating quality. Next year, wholesalers wrote 'Please send hail-pitted apples if possible, otherwise ship regular kind.' This is a true story.

A French manufacturer of fashion garments made of natural fibre had a similar problem. They wrinkled when washed. So he sewed on a tag 'Guaranteed to wrinkle.' (Does Levi still advertise jeans 'Guaranteed to shrink and fade?')

2. Provided the product does the job, all other attributes of product quality are merely in the mind. This does not make them less real or important to the buyer.

For example, cosmetic manufacturers know well that a low priced cosmetic can be a disaster. Otherwise, everyone would buy their cosmetics from Boots. 'If it doesn't sell, raise the price' may be a vulgar way of putting it, but those who successfully market luxury goods at 1000 per cent-plus margins have proven that price is one, and sometimes the only, index of perceived quality.

A notorious few of Britain's largest PR consultancies charge outrageously high hourly fees. These bear no relation to their costs or performance. Why? It attracts the largest clients, who would not feel comfortable paying lower fees or going 'out of town', even for demonstrably superior services. Too often where intangible services are concerned, like consultancy, high price is the only tangible assurance the customer has of quality. Or at least, it is the only assurance he can give his Board . . .

So why fight it? Try *increasing* your price – or better, launching your product at the very top of the market. If anyone makes awkward price/benefit comparisons with your competitors, point to your list of very satisfied customers and say 'Obviously, our clients believe that you get what you pay for.'

I am assuming, of course, that your product actually

does the job. Marketing schlock at luxury prices is a fast way to bankruptcy!

3. Another way to overcome potential objections to what may, at first, appear to be a lower quality product is to ask customers: 'Why pay for what you don't need?'

One Guild delegate had the task of promoting a personal computer. It did nothing that others didn't, and did them rather slower. It had only one output port, compared with two or three offered by the market leaders. Its saving grace was its low price – but then the market could boast plenty of price bargains.

So he promoted the single port as a benefit. The firm had genuinely found that most pc users wanted only one port anyway, to drive a printer; few in this price band really needed electronic mail or distributed processing. So its successful theme became 'All that you need, for less'.

4. Remember that 'lower quality' may be only in your *own* mind. Occasionally the prospect really does want just the fundamentals. Remember the Volkswagen ads? And their disarming single-word headline 'Lemon'? And the copy which confessed 'It's ugly, but it gets you there'? Thousands of students, low-income housewives and civil servants sympathised with that approach . . . and bought Volkswagen.

7

ZEN AND THE ART OF AD LAYOUT

'Of ad copywriters, there are three kinds: apprentices, journeymen and masters. The first attend award dinners. The second go to receive the awards. But master copy-smiths send their regrets, from the Bahamas. They're far too busy to attend.' Copywriter, Nick van Rijn.

van Rijn is wrong, of course. No copywriter today with any sensibility lives in the Bahamas. But he's right when he goes on to say that ads are 'creative', only if they sell product.

Creativity in advertising has just two roles: to increase the numbers who will read the ad, and those who will act on it. To generate volumes of valid sales leads, you need highly responsive ads.

Designer ads provoke your response: 'What an ad! I must congratulate the designer.' But responsive ads challenge you: 'What an ad! I must buy that product.' This is why the 'borrowed interest' ad fails: the shock headline, the irrelevantly glamorous model girl, the jokey teaser.

Unless your ad answers at once, 'What's in it for me?' you've lost the reader. And the sale. Of course, it pays to use a professional. But if your budget demands you design your own ad (or you must monitor the ads your agency presents) here are some tips that make it simpler. (I'm indebted to the advice of copywriter extraordinaire, Alastair Crompton for many of these thoughts):

1.   Avoid using a big layout pad for your scribbles. It's deceptive. Instead, draw a space exactly the same size as the space you're buying. That way, you're less likely to try to squeeze in War and Peace – and if you do, it becomes obvious that a typeface smaller than 9 point just isn't going to be legible anyway.

2.   Headlines below the illustration are read by 10 per cent more people than headlines above the illustration, saith David Ogilvy. (Where *did* he get these fascinating figures? And why doesn't he share his sources with us? Could it be that, heaven forfend, he *made them up*?)

But in this case he's right. Many surveys confirm that readers look at the picture first, then the headline, then the picture caption, then the bottom of the page (to check the price and who's advertising), and then the subheads (to get a quick scan of the contents). All in a few seconds. They may then start to read the body copy, but only if you're very lucky. Merely 5 per cent of those who notice your ad, will go on to read the small print.

So put your most impactful selling points in that order of priority. Picture, headline, caption, subheads, sign-off . . . And remember that the photo should illustrate the key *benefit* (it should not exist just to support the headline). So the photo caption should powerfully convey a benefit too. It should not merely be a label. (You do have a caption, don't you?)

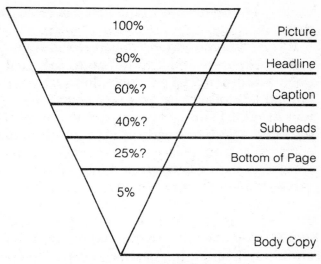

How readers fall away as they read your ad

3. Moreover, Ogilvy claims that headlines set in quotation marks have a 28 per cent greater recall than those set without quotation marks. (Sounds reasonable. Observe how many newspaper headlines are set in quotes . . . although these rarely bear much resemblance to what the quoted person actually said.) If you can't quote a third party, quote yourself – or lift a gobbet of text from your own 'body copy' i.e. the small print of your ad.

And don't put a full stop after your headline. The last thing you want now is for the reader to stop!

4. Ensure your reader's eye movements follow a logical order, top to bottom, left to right. That's the way most of us are taught to read. The bottom right-hand corner is the place to put your company name, telephone number and call to action. Because that's where you Take the

Order . . . and it's one of the first places the reader's eye rests.

If you use a coupon, try to book a right-hand page, and put your coupon in the bottom right-hand corner. (If you book a left-hand page, you must put your coupon at bottom left: otherwise you lose responses. Few readers will struggle to insert scissors to cut a coupon positioned next to the 'gutter' or crease. Amazingly, some ads have coupons in the *middle* of the page!) If you're not sure which side your coupon will fall, lay the coupon right across the bottom of the page.

5. Use narrow columns, around 40 characters or 8 words wide. Avoid setting entire words in capital letters, and do not set your headline in capitals. They stop the eye travelling and lose readers. Have you ever seen a newspaper set small text in capitals? They don't, because they know that capital letters erect picket fences, shedding readers at every jump.

Drop in a subhead between the headline and the body copy, to tease the reader over that awful bridge of white space. (Remember, readers can't read white spaces.)

Visualise your paragraphs . . . and your subheads, illustrations and graphic details as components which are intended to *unbalance* your reader! Now that's heresy, so let me explain . . .

The last thing you want is a perfectly 'balanced' layout! You can observe the balanced mortuary-slab approach in any corporate brochure. Everything is of equal size and shape. All is slick. So nothing is read.

Instead, you want variety, excitement and lots of nasty 'hooks' – calculated imperfections – on the page, to arrest the reader's eye and guide his pen to your response device! Unless, of course, you are selling funeral services. But even then . . .

Of course, you can overdo this, and end up with another sort of designer-ad – irrelevant excitement, and nowhere a benefit. Rather, what I mean is best illustrated by the finesse of the Zen master. Take a perfect layout, and find three elements you can judiciously 'spoil'. Twist a photo out of kilter. Omit a key word and 'write' it back in with a blue pen. Scrub out one price or benefit and overlay it visibly with an improved one.

Only now is it perfect (i.e. credible because touched by human hand, and responsive). This is not at all the same as achieving imperfections by accident . . .

6. Ogilvy claims that a drop initial at start of the text (i.e. a big letter that descends to two or three lines) boosts readership by 13 per cent. Who am I to argue?

8

HOW TO USE ILLUSTRATIONS TO IMPROVE SALES RESPONSE

1. Photographs in your ads imply authenticity. Particularly colour photos. It's the way the world looks. But don't use groups or montages. Readers identify with individuals, not with mobs. Photos are valuable in *large* newspaper and magazine ads, and brochures – but don't use them in small ads or directories, where the poor reproduction quality or small size available may make a nonsense of them. In these cases, use line illustration.

2. 'Colour photos outpull black-and-white by 200 per cent', is the traditional wisdom. *It's not always true . . .* Yes, colour imports prestige. It implies a costly production process. But this may bore the ad-sophisticates on the one hand, and irritate advertising-haters on the other.

Remember that charities invariably get better results with black and white photos, the grainier the better.

If *you* want to convey down-to-earth Honesty, Sincerity and the Personal touch, go for black and white photos. If you don't, use colour.

3. Rectangular photos outpull square ones: they are more interesting to the eye. They also reinforce our dictums referred to above (and proved in practice) on Zen and the Art of Ad Layout. *Calculated* imperfection – of whatever kind – pulls a better response.

4. Most photos can and should be improved with a little artwork – such as, gently airbrushing to sharpen the contrast or to reduce a confusing background. Or scalpel work to cut a head-and-shoulders into sharp profile. Budget for this.

5. If the product is visually unexciting, show the *application* not the product. Picture credible individuals enjoying the benefits. Depict the finished result – not the ingredients.

For example, suppose you're advertising a muesli product on an 18-foot wide poster on the London Underground. Would you show a delicious bowl of muesli adorned with luscious fruit? Or a grotty pile of dried oats? No prizes for the answer. Yet inexplicably an ad agency spent a megabudget doing the latter, under the benefit-free catchline 'Body maintenance by Jordans.' Jordans are a lovely company who market those delicious crunchy bars. They deserved better . . .

6. If the product or service is intangible – like software, or plant maintenance, or consultancy – show a diagram, a graphic, a bar chart, *anything* to make the product tangible and illustrate the benefits.

One of my marketing consultancy clients is a top-name business translation service. How do you illustrate translation?

Photos of bemused foreigners boggling at your trade show are *not* the way. Instead, we devised a simple diagram, a flow-chart, which showed first, the stages of misunderstanding which could result from a *poor* translation. It started with 'Maybe this company could help us' and descended through levels of bafflement and despair to 'Maybe I should hire these clowns for my son's barmitzvah?'

Secondly, we showed another flow chart. It illustrated the patient steps of quality control which our client exerted – specifically to avoid snafus like that.

7.   If the product's benefits are hidden, use a cutaway diagram to show the working parts. But flag each part, with a caption describing – not just its function – but its benefit to the reader.

THE TRUTH ABOUT THE OGILVY SQUARES

David Ogilvy developed a 'house style', which he used for everything from Hathaway shirts to British tourism. It created rules which many ad agencies have since forgotten, and was immensely successful. If you want to be another Ogilvy, why struggle to re-invent the wheel? Here are his 'tested layouts'. If you use them, I'm sure he'll love you . . .

The Portrait format
This is characterised by a big photograph which occupies the whole top two-thirds of the space. (For this you need

a whole page or large portrait-sized equivalent space.)

It's a colour photo (because Ogilvy believes this has double the impact of black-and-white. Ho, hum . . .).

Immediately under it is a long headline, set in lower case type. There is no period at the end. It probably begins: Why . . . How . . . When . . . Where . . . (These are proven editorial devices to lead the reader in to the body copy. Check your last edition of Readers Digest . . .)

Sometimes after this long headline, there's a second headline, also in lower case. This is set in smaller type and possibly underlined. (Another editorial device, which acts as a bridge into the body copy.)

The body copy is then set in two or three columns, no wider than 40 characters. First letter is a large 'drop letter'. Copy follows the rules of good newspaper writing: short words (max three syllables), short sentences (max twenty words), short paragraphs (max three sentences). Several sub-heads break up the text, and act as 'flags' which lead the eye on. The sub-heads summarise key benefits.

At the end of the copy, is a Call to Action. 'Do this . . . send this . . . remember this . . . look for this product in the store . . .'

It may show a small picture of the product at the bottom right (pictures draw the eye, and the last paragraph is where you make the sale). It may even have a PS repeating the most important benefit or the reason to act now, as if this were a personal letter. (And isn't it?)

The Landscape format
In this case, the photo is set left, occupying the whole depth. At right, the copy follows the same format as the

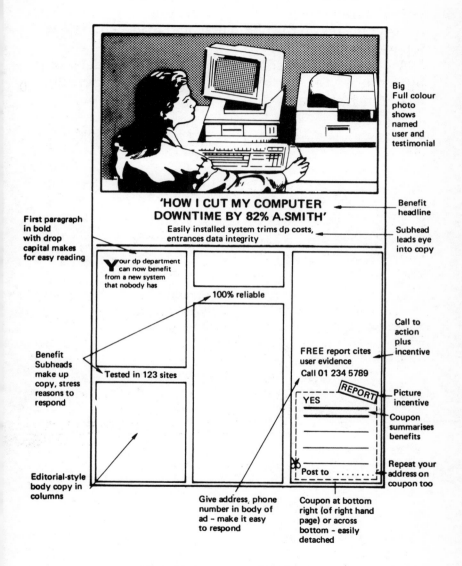

Model layout for a responsive ad

portrait format above. (This is the natural progression for the eye. It fixes on the photo first, and reads left to right, top to bottom.)

Are these formulas? Yes. Is it wrong to be hidebound by formulas? Yes. Do they work? Does David Ogilvy live in a French chateau?

9

SUCCEED WITH NEWSPAPER ADS

The design of 'direct response' advertising is a precise science. Precise, in the sense that, if you get it wrong, you can test and test, until you get it right – or your budget runs out. It is the only style of advertising you should be using, if you have a small budget. Even if you *don't* want a direct response. Why? Because the rules have been honed by experience to gain you the maximum reader impact and involvement at minimum cost. What you then do with that impact, is up to you!

You will find detailed suggestions on direct response ads elsewhere in this book; here are a few which apply particularly to newspapers.

1.   Put your most powerful benefit in the headline. Plus your name. After all, four out of five people who even scan your ad will not read any further. (Yes, I've said that before. It's worth repeating.) Here's a powerful idea: put the name of your town in the heading, if you want impact. ('Calling Luton men with chilblains! Smithy's lotion gives instant relief . . .')

In the US, there are virtually no national newspapers.

So advertisers take volumes of local press ads, nation-wide. To ensure response, they prepare identical tested artwork – but they change each headline to target the paper's hometown ('Calling Chicago men with chilblains!' etc).

2. Put your other key benefits in subheads.

3. Illustrate your product or service *being enjoyed by a typical customer*. Women identify with women, men with men, etc. If you want to reach mothers, show babies. If older people are your target show puppies. A horrid generalisation and crass, 'tis true. But it works.
    Beware of the awful reproduction of most newspapers: small detail and subtle tone gradations in photos will be lost.

4. Write long copy. In fact, consider using all-editorial format. Conventional wisdom says it typically outpulls response to display ads by six to one. My own repeated experience suggests this is, if anything, a gross understatement.

5. If using mostly editorial format, write a long headline. If you must make it short, use huge letters. But in lower case. Try to include the word 'Free'.

6. Put your address, phone number and ideally a tollfree (LinkLine) number at bottom. Make responding easy. Mention credit cards you honour. Do *not* put your address on the coupon alone: (a) it's questionable practice under mail order laws; (b) how will customers contact you, if they've already sent off/lost the coupon?

Repeat your address and full response information in the body of the ad.

7. Create urgency. 'Discount must end by January 30th', 'your last chance this year'.

8. Give an extra incentive to respond. 'Bring in this ad for a free gift', 'Drive in now for your free Report on How to Winterize your Car'.

You will get respondees who appear to be time-wasters, i.e. they do not convert to business at once. Don't despair. Keep mailing them. Most respondees are saying 'Yes, I'm interested in your product – just don't pressure me yet.'

9. Set the ad in a heavy border, particularly if small.

10. Consider a brochure or handbill insert into your local newspaper. It costs slightly more than an ad, but usually gets a far better response. It falls out when the newspaper is opened and draws attention to itself. It is often kept when the newspaper itself is trashed. And it can even be a low-cost pull of your existing artwork.

By selecting the newspaper you go into, you can achieve some quite sophisticated media targeting. There are nationwide household distribution services, including the Post Office, who will arrange selective doordrops like this, for a fee. But your newsagent may do it for you on a local level, unofficially, just for petty cash.

11. Test every ad. Compare different headlines, offers. Code them. Calculate percentage response rates over a period. Note seasonal dips and peaks. Test different days of the week. (Monday is often good for male readers, checking the weekend sports results. Thursday/ Friday is traditionally good for food ads. National and regional Sundays are legendary for family offers, leisure, holidays and luxury items.)

Over 12 months, this log should become a priceless planning guide, directing your expenditure over the next year.

10

THREE WAYS TO MULTIPLY YOUR RESPONSE FROM PRINT ADS

A little imitation envelope was stuck to the page of my *Sunday Times* magazine. 'Tear this . . . you'll find it's tough!' it said. I did. It was. Behind it on the page, which advertised super-tough envelopes, was a reply coupon. The envelope could have doubled as a reply device too. Alas, it didn't, but . . .

1. . . . it illustrates the value of the *tip-on*, a card (or sample, or other attention-getter) lightly affixed with gum, which makes your passive ad powerfully interactive. 'Touch me', it says. 'Test me. Now we have a dialogue going, send me back (complete with your name, address, even your payment).'

It works. Moben Kitchens routinely tip on a separate reply card in their print ads, above and additional to the reply coupon. Obviously, it costs them (around £40 per 1,000). Obviously, it works (they've been doing it a long time). It has the added advantage, that it doubles the reply opportunity (Reader X returns the card, and the printed coupon's still there to entice Reader Y). But how can you and I, on limited budgets, explore this principle?

2. Answer: *multiply* the opportunity for readers to respond. Include a reply coupon *plus* your normal office telephone number *plus* a 'hotline' 24-hour answering machine for credit card orders or enquiries. One tollfree system is LinkLine (works like magic with consumer ads, less well – but still worth testing – in business-to-business ads. Call your British Telecom sales office).

3. Turn your ad into a novel *self-mailer*. Instead of booking a double-page spread, which (commonsense suggests) will be flipped over as one unit and not be read, take the *front* and *back* of just one page. Insist each side faces editorial (at once, you get 150 per cent-plus more readers). Design the *bottom* halves of page one and two as a back-to-back self-mailing coupon. Complete, cut, fold and tuck. No stamp needed.

That latter idea will horrify your ad designer (it's so inelegant!). But it's novel enough to be worth a try. I'll wager it will please your bank manager.

11

HOW TO GET QUALIFIED SALES LEADS FROM CLASSIFIED ADS – THAT MAY COST YOU LITTLE OR NOTHING TO GET

When mega-budget competitors have, so to speak, dynamited the fishpond, some wily advertisers prefer to tickle their trout into the net. They use a three-step sales vehicle:

1. First, they place – and test – lots of small classifieds. Each offers a *free* report with a carefully and very specifically defined title: 'How to save money when selling your house', 'Five ways to cut computer downtime in insurance applications', etc. This eliminates most enquirers who are not in their market.

In consumer journals, they often ask for a postage stamp to deter the freebie collectors – but if you want to do this, test how this affects your response (and conversion to sale).

2. Second, respondents receive a full direct mail package with their free report (this is usually an inexpensive eight-page DL-sized booklet, the size of a normal office envelope). The package either sells the offer there and then, or contains a reply card offering information. This is followed up by a telephone call to schedule a visit by the sales rep or dealer.

3. Conversions to sale from Step 2 can be 10 per cent or more – enough to pay for the promotion. But the *real* profits are made from steps 3 through 10: *the repeated mailing of your prospects with different offers, until either they buy or reach the threshold of non-profitability.*

Some catalogue advertisers even expect to make a loss on their first order from a new customer. Why? They are more concerned with securing the customer's loyalty, so they can profitably 'back sell'. To this end, they will often give gifts with the first order, or 'love' tokens. These are free products that the customer did not expect, but they say 'Thank you for your business'.

The lifetime value of the customer – in repeated purchases – may far outweigh the loss made on the first order. Seasoned direct mailers call this loss the 'acquisition cost.'

4. Finally, the shrewd marketer recoups much of his promotional costs – by renting out his enquiry lists to other direct mail promoters.

For example, your customer list (enquiries converted to sale) might rent at £95 per 1000 or more. Rates of £150 per 1000 or more are not uncommon for proven responsive lists. Your enquiry list (not yet converted) might rent at a lower figure, say at £55 per 1000.

If you have under 5000 names, write direct to non-competitive marketing firms who might be interested in your list (or will swop lists with you). If you have over 5000 names, a list broker will be interested. He'll take 20 per cent commission for every rental, but can ensure your list is rented time and again.

Fallacies about list rental
So you're not too happy about renting out your list. Why?

a) 'My list will get "used up" by other firms renting it, even if they offer non-competing products.' Wrong! Strong evidence exists that the more times your list is rented, the better *your* subsequent returns from it. It seems people need to be 'educated' into responding by mail. It's addictive. The more they do it, the more they want to. You will normally *improve* your list.

b) 'It will be stolen'. Wrong! Make sure your list is entrusted only to a reputable mailing house – a BDMA member, who is governed by professional codes (fierce, with exemplary teeth to them) to guard against just this. The organisation which rents your list need never see it. And seed your list with decoys – names of your neighbours or friends. Let list renters know your list is seeded with decoys.

If they misuse your list (unlikely), you can now legally demand damages. However, this is a bit like slamming shut the stable door, if someone has already bolted with your list. So why not insist that – instead of sending off your list – you receive the renter's promotional pieces and you'll mail them. (For example, many publishers do this. They refuse to release the names on their own promotional list, recognising this is their lifeblood.) You can then pack them at a mailing house of your choice. Add your margin to the mailing house's charges, and you could profit again.

c) 'It will be over-used'. Lucky you! The more times it's

used, the more money you make – and the more responsive it (often) becomes. See (a) above.

The result of your multi-step plan is that, not only can you make a profit on direct sales, but also you recoup – over a period – the cost of getting your sales leads. By renting the names continuously to others! (Some very astute marketers advertise *solely* 'free information' to gain leads in this way – yet have no product to sell. They still profit, because they rent out the names they gain. These can be defined very closely by the enquirers' field of interest, making them valuable to other mailing companies.)

However, be aware that the Data Protection Act has now imposed certain constraints on the use of your mailing list by third parties. Check the latest guidelines with the Data Protection Registrar, Springfield House, Water Lane, Wilmslow, Cheshire SK9 5AX. Phone 0625-535711.

76

12

CLASSIFIED ADS – HOW TO PACK POWER
INTO A TINY SPACE

Do classified ads work? Check the business columns of
The Mail or *Sunday Times* over several months, and count
how often the same ads reappear. Obviously, they are
making money. And they can be your cheapest form of
advertising, outpulling display ads. This is particularly
true of recruitment ads, up to middle manager level.

The Times' personal columns (classifieds) are one of its
best read sections, even scanned by other newspapers
for news stories!

To get the best out of classifieds, ask yourself these
questions:

1. *Decide why you are using classifieds.*
(a) To generate leads? Then, do not expect to sell 'off the
page' – you do not have enough space to paint a full
enough picture for prospects to send you money, sometimes not even a postage stamp to pay for your reply.
Instead, classifieds can generate sales leads – to which
you bounce back your direct mail package or full brochure, and that brings the order or appointment with
your sales rep as above.

(b) To test – inexpensively – headlines, benefits, claims? Don't overlook this simple method of copy testing. Once you have a 'benchmark' figure for response from a series of identical ads, you can easily – and quickly – test different headline or copy changes by *running them as classifieds*. If the lineage ad pulls, chances are its equivalent will pull in a display ad. But remember to 'key' each ad, for example Dept ST12 in the address could indicate 12th insertion, *Sunday Times*.

2. *Should you run short classified ads because everyone else does?*
No! Instead, run long classifieds. They'll be more responsive, for the same reason that long sales letters outpull short ones. Serious prospects will read every word, several times. Inspect the ads that appear, unchanged every week, in *Exchange & Mart*. Obviously, they work. And some are several hundred words long.

3. *Should your classifieds read more like a letter than an ad?*
Write the copy in the same way as a direct mail letter – it's a far more personal message than a display ad. Emphasise 'I' and 'You'; paint word pictures of benefits; use the 'power' words like 'free', 'guarantee'. (See the section on writing ads and direct mail.)

4. *What will best pull the reader's eye?*
Write a short benefit-packed headline, and pay extra to list it bold in capitals. A variation on this is to run a series of short teaser headlines in bold, down one column. They are interspersed by other people's ads. The reader thus has several chances to see your teaser. And the payoff comes in your last ad, which reveals the full offer.

The one liners build a consecutive teaser message, and the punch line comes at the bottom. For example, 'Want variety? Think Brown'/'Want responsibility? Think Brown'/'Want a career? Think Brown.'/'Want to know more? Brown offers you all this . . .' 'Splitting your copy down the column this way costs very little more, but packs a big impact.

5. *Should you go for semi-display?*
Frame your ad in a heavy solid box. Or perhaps run your headline in a panel, white out of black. (For this you will need to pay more, to prepare your own artwork. You can't trust the journal to do it right.)
But do not reverse out your main text. It will be virtually impossible to read. And avoid too many wobs (white out of blacks). They can make an ad look schlocky.

6. *Can you run a classified campaign?*
Once you've tested a given journal, buy a series to gain heavy discounts. Then vary the ads each week so they cycle through, for example, four creative variations. Repeat indefinitely, or until falling response tells you to try a new creative approach. Keep the main benefit identical (unless you are deliberately testing different benefits). In this way, your creative classified ads can in time create awareness as well as response, even a cult following!

13

HOW TO TURN YOUR DIRECTORY ADS INTO SALES LEAD-GETTERS

Yellow Pages and their many variants are often the first resource of customers – even major prospects for business-to-business sales. My own marketing consultancy has gained at least three very large clients in as many years, through 'bluebird' responses to our local Yellow Page ads. (A 'bluebird' is an unexpected sale which just flew in the door.)

But most directory ads appear to be a mere labelling exercise, a token effort, as if the advertiser never expected them to win business – a self-fulfilling prophecy.

Yet organisations trading in a local market *must* exploit Yellow Page-type ads, which include Thomson regional directories (particularly if you want to reach consumers) and British Telecom's Business Pages (if you sell business-to-business). Directories are the main source of business for most plumbers, tv repair shops, vehicle breakdown services . . . even retailers. Why?

The majority of customers for an independent store live no more than a quarter-mile away – while even a shopping centre gains 90 per cent of its customers within a four-mile radius. With the exception of highly specialist stores, or those selling mainly by mail-order, this rule will apply to virtually any trader orientated to the local market.

Apparently, 96 per cent of telephone subscribers refer to Yellow Pages. Three out of four consult them by making a phone call, one in ten make a personal visit, and more than one in two buy something as a result.

Of course, you get a free listing in the Yellow Pages if you have a business telephone. But so do your competitors. You must outsell them. How to do it?

1. *Run a press or radio or poster ad and tell people to 'find you in Yellow Pages'?*
Sure they will, along with all your competitors. You'll spend money, just to give your business to the opposition. Refer them in your advertising, if you must, but to your boldface listing in the *white* pages.

Better, give them your phone number then and there. Better still, make sure it's a LinkLine or Freephone number – highly memorable, and it costs them nothing to call. (Details from your telephone sales office.) Almost certainly, your competition won't be offering that.

2. *Take the largest display ad you can afford.*
Most customers will call *only* those with prominent ads. A bold-face listing is better than nothing, but a listing alone is almost worthless.

In directories, every advertiser has the same restrictions of space and reproduction quality, and competes on equal terms. This is your chance to trounce the market leader with a power-packed ad.

'Best buys' are bottom third of page or full length of

right hand column, with the telephone listings above or alongside.

3. *Don't be shy.*
Remember that everyone scanning a directory is a *hot prospect*. They have a problem or need right now. So your ad should sell its heart out.

4. *Specify layouts that gain extra impact.*
Avoid fine-line artwork: go for bold graphics, reversed-out headlines, heavy 12-point frames with your text inset surrounded by white space: this will draw the reader's eye like the proverbial magnet.

Print your telephone number very, very big and try to get one that's memorable. Freephone numbers are memorable because they are remembered by names, not numbers. But . . . you'll also lose calls because impatient callers won't wait for the operator to answer. The virtue of Freephone's rival – LinkLine – is that callers dial you direct, at no cost to themselves. But the service is pricey and impossible to test on a very small budget.

Some independent local directories incorporate money-off coupons. Try them: they're 'time tested' in the US as potent sales lead-pullers. Some directories offer colour. If yours is the only colour ad on the page (and well composed), it will steal the available business. Go for it.

5. *Avoid adland clichés.*
Yellow Pages bristle with nonsense phrases like 'Big enough to serve, small enough to care'; 'The best in (xxx)'; 'Quality service at competitive rates'; 'For all your (xxx) needs'; etc. Instead, find the one proposition which will break your ad out from the competition, and

highlight it. This could be as simple as a tollfree LinkLine telephone number 'call us now – FREE!'

6. *Illustrate your product or service.*
. . . and picture your typical customer enjoying its benefits. Simple line graphics. Low cost. Obvious, but very rarely done.

7. *Detail what your customer must do to get the benefits.*
Call you, sure. But do you offer a 24-hour enquiry service? (Most 24-hour personal answering services are priced only for megabudget national promotions. Instead, hitch up a telephone answering machine, and promise to call them back. You'll lose orders from those with machine-phobia. But you'll gain some, too – because your competitors will not have offered this simple convenience.)

8. *List benefits, benefits, benefits.*
No matter if your ad looks 'busy', or overfull. Hot prospects will read every word. Make it personal: 'you' and 'I' language. Follow the rules for writing: remember the power of the word 'Free'. Do you take credit cards? If so, specify them. Be specific: list your opening times, your discount range, number of satisfied customers each year. (But you'll have to prove any such claims on demand, and you're stuck with them for a year.)

Remember that directory scanners generally seek three things: *fast* telephone response (they have a problem now, and they won't call back if you're engaged or not answering); response *today* (be sure to mention if you're open 7 days, or 12 hours a day); and *reassurance* of your bona fides (they probably don't know you, yet they're entrusting you with their problem).

So reassure them. Mention your membership of trade associations, the years you or your firm, or the years collectively that your staff, have been in the business, your guarantee – but only if it can be phrased accurately in a few words e.g. 'Your job done in one day or no charge'.

9. *Consider running several ads . . .*
if you have several strong sales points, for example 24-hour enquiry service, or free delivery, or easy credit terms. Particularly, run two ads – or at least, bold face listings – if yours is a name that could be spelled or looked up in different ways. Would they look for 'A A Smithy' under A or S? Make sure you appear in both places.

Airline Qantas is wisely listed in the London telephone directory under Quantas and Qantas. Could you benefit from this idea?

And if your business could be described under different categories, of course you should consider listing there as well. Multiple listings also qualify for discounts.

10. *Avoid humour – puns, jokes, cartoons.*
People do not scan directory pages for pleasure. They have a problem. They do *not* have time to puzzle out your joke. (This advice could apply to virtually any ad!) They want a serious reason to call you now – or they'll turn to the next ad.

This advice is true also for trade directories. Readers do *not* browse through them like a magazine. For example, editorial articles in these directories are simply not read. Ignore any publisher who asks you to submit, say, a 2000 word feature for 'free inclusion' in your own trade's directory! It isn't worth the time spent picking up your pen.

11. *Monitor your enquiries from directories.*
– and anywhere else. Ask 'Where did you hear about us?' Make sure the switchboard asks the source of the sales lead, if no one else is around to capture the enquiry.

Of course, enquirers will always reply unhelpfully 'I saw the ad'. But you can still track the source by putting in your ad different names: 'Call Brenda Brown on 01–234 5678'. If enquirers ask the switchboard for Brenda Brown, that's code B. (Of course, you don't have a Brenda Brown, but the switchboard puts them through to 'Brenda Brown's department' or 'Ann Adams' or 'Carol Clark', etc, meaning codes A or C respectively.)

A big no, no: Do not let the directory people write your ad.

14

GET VALUE FROM LOCAL RADIO ADS

Many marketers neglect the potential of local radio as a source of useful sales leads. Perhaps because it is literally 'less visible' as a marketing vehicle than trade press or newspapers. Also Britain is less well served than, say, the US where no fewer than 10,000 radio stations exist, and the ratio is one station per 26,500 people. Our ratio is more like one station per 520,000.

Yet radio can drive in enquiries and customers, even in business-to-business markets, if you observe these – often little regarded – rules:

1. Recognise that the degree of impact of your ad is in inverse ratio to the amount of music run by the programme. Music stations are 'wallpaper' stations – they create an environment, present but only intermittently attended to. However, talk stations – or those with a large number of talk programmes – aggressively demand listeners' attention. Subject to the aptness of your offer, they could provide a higher response per pound spent.

2. Know that peak radio listening is at morning and

evening drive times, and that people are more receptive in the evening drive after work. But don't expect a motorist to reach for a pencil and write down your phone number.

Use of a memorable Freephone number, such as 'Freephone Help' for a windscreen replacement service, is better than a number alone. But if you must cite a telephone number, use it at least three times during the ad: the first time to tell people it's coming, the second to drive them to a pencil, and the third to remind them what you said.

And *don't* conceal the number with overly heavy background music or obtrusive sound effects.

If you want *response*, as opposed merely to a large audience, do not book at prime times such as the 'drive' times or in the news or soap opera programmes. Listeners are too absorbed to reach for a pen, to note your name. Instead, try off-peak time – even late at night. It has higher response. And because its audience is smaller, you pay less per sales lead. Two out of three radio ads run by Procter & Gamble in the US are in daytime and fringe time. Procter & Gamble is a £10 billion company.

3. Build on the radio station's own credibility – see if the announcer will sample your product, then report on it. Perhaps ad lib a 'commercial'?

When my consultancy launched a (now) well-known muesli bar, we mailed samples to BBC radio DJs. Two of the best known interspersed their commentary with apologies for the crunching noises on mike, named the bar and volunteered healthy approval. And we hadn't even paid for the air time!

Radio is one of those few occasions when it pays to get the radio station to produce your ad, if you're working to a tiny budget.

4. Fifteen second spots are usually the costliest per second, but are the most economical in the long run, in series bookings.

Note there are two kinds of ad: if you want to reach as many people as possible, say, with a Reminder or News ad ('just two more days left to claim your luxury fur coat for just £50' or 'We open today – come and claim your free £50 voucher') little and often is better than a few biggies. These will each reach only a tiny part of the listening audience. But if you want direct response ('call this number now') you probably need a much longer ad to pack the persuasive power – plus repetition – you need to drive in enquiries.

5. Use interesting sounds. Music is a natural, ideally a unique tune which you play over and over as your theme. Remember the Esso Blue tune? It's sixteen years since last it was played, yet still old-timers among us find ourselves whistling it! (Beware the Screech Effect or SE. Anyone who has nearly lost control of a car, when a piercingly loud blast of music emanated from a radio commercial, will understand that SEs are counter-productive.)

But individual signature tunes cost megabudgets. How can you afford the upfront cost of your own tune? Strike a deal with a composer. He'll compose you a unique tune. You'll rent its use from him on a monthly basis. A year later, if your advertising has worked, you'll buy it from him. If not, it's his to resell.

Does this sound odd? It's commonplace – and not just for music. (A similar rent-or-buy deal works well for us, in respect of uniquely-titled Award schemes or Surveys or Conferences or other promotions we devise for our clients. We do the development work. They can rent the scheme's use to promote their own name, with the option to buy or cancel at year-end as their budget allows. If necessary, we can then resell the concept elsewhere.)

6. Don't use professional celebrities. Their cost is stratospheric, and their credibility arguable. Today's public are getting cynical about patently commercial endorsements. Far better is to hire a professional interviewer, perhaps a 'name' newscaster, to interview *you* – or your company chief executive. If the latter sounds like the second coming of Dracula, use a professional actor who is introduced as a 'company spokesman'.

The happy result is, no breathless hype from a plastic announcer. Just facts from a friend. Well edited, it can sound like a local news bulletin – instantly credible *and listened to*. Even better, is to co-opt a local hero – such as a recently celebrated sports star. Topical, convincing and inexpensive. But be fast. He is already signing up with an agent, and will never be as cheap again. Better still is to interview a satisfied named customer. If you can, ask him to co-fund your ad, particularly if you both address the same market. Won't it boost *his* stock in the market too?

LBC listeners were recently surprised to hear jazz luminary Ronnie Scott endorsing a department store. Ingenuously, he explained that he was only doing the ad because it gave him a chance to plug his jazz club – which he then did. Why not likewise explore joint ads with other advertisers – even luminaries – as a way to cut costs, and boost your credibility?

7. Remember that radio – used on its own – works most cost-effectively as a Reminder ('We're the big red building in Petticoat Lane', 'Our sale has only 24 hours to go – so call in today!'), or a News vehicle ('We're giving away 10 per cent on prices of all our new cars, starting today!') or as Information ('Here are the temperatures today in the sunspots of Europe' – from a travel agency). Ideally, people should already know where and who you are.

Unless you want to gamble big, radio is *not* the most profitable place to launch a new product from an unknown firm – or to ask for the order outright.

8. Which begs the question, why use radio on its own? It becomes really effective in driving in sales leads, if you marry it with other media.

One of my clients mailed a simple letter to his prospects in one radio region. He urged, tune in to my radio ad. Why? It contained the first three digits of a postcode, allegedly picked at random by his computer. (The right three digits can encompass several hundred prospect companies.) If your office was located in that postcode area, he said, you won a big prize. But you had to phone his office next day – and answer some simple questions about your qualifications to purchase – to collect your prize.

Some folk might argue that his approach was not strictly legal. It seems you are supposed to restrict your prize values in schemes like this to £1, at least on tv commercials. (Radio is a grey area, simply because hardly anyone else has tried this scheme yet, and radio sales reps can usually see no objections. French viewers are luckier; the legal prize ceiling is £3000.)

But let's be safe, and restrict our prize to (say) a modest A3-size aerial map of the postcode region, ready for framing, and featuring the prospect's office (net cost per photocopy, under £1). It's still a novel prize, and you have the bonus of offering to hand-deliver it, framed, to suitably qualifying respondents.

That's the way to make radio profitable, in your sales lead generation programme!

CHECK IF YOUR DRAFT AD OR BROCHURE IS
RESPONSIVE – BEFORE YOU RUN IT

There is no substitute to actually running an ad, to tell if it will work. But you can at least test if your ad will be understood – and is making the best use of its budget, *before* running it, in these four ways:

Test One (3 seconds)
Give it to a friend to read – someone not familiar with your business. After three seconds take it back.
   Ask – what is the ad selling? What is the main benefit it offers? What must the reader do to get this benefit? What was your initial emotional response – bored, provoked, or interested? If you get the right answers, proceed to two.

Test Two (10 seconds)
Cover up the body copy, leaving only the headlines, subheads, photos, graphic elements and captions visible.
   Give them 10 seconds. Ask – is enough information and benefits still conveyed, for the reader to understand your offer and to respond? If so, that's a good ad!

If your draft has passed those tests, it's time to refine it. Now apply this 60-second test:

Test Three (60 seconds)
Is the main benefit stated in the headline? Is it shown in the main illustration? Does the illustration caption reinforce the main benefit? Is it immediately obvious what you're selling?

Does the headline grab the reader? Is the impact relevant and appropriate? Or . . .

. . . have you mugged the reader with Irrelevant Impact ('FREE MONEY! Now that we have your attention, let's change the subject and talk about our product . . .')?

Or have you hit the reader with the wet sponge of Whimsical Creativity? (This is easy to tell. If your reader's first response is likely to be 'how clever/cute this ad is' rather than 'I want it now!' – it's probably a 'designer ad'. It will appeal only to art directors. Who have no money.)

Is every feature translated into a benefit? Are secondary benefits emphasised in sub-heads?

Are your words one or two syllables, sentences no more than twenty words, paragraphs no longer than seven lines?

Have you made any unsubstantiated claims? Used generalities? (Check for words like 'many', 'biggest', 'best', 'lowest price': then justify them with figures or third-party proof.) Have you stretched the truth? Does it sound honest and credible?

Does the layout flag the reader's path top-to-bottom, left-to-right – leading him effortlessly through to the action point (telephone number, coupon, whatever)? Or is it cluttered? Does the eye have to backtrack? Can readers easily understand what they must now do?

Test Four (30 minutes)
If you're budgeting more than, say, £50,000 (and even if you're not) you'll profit by another test. Take three or four versions of your intended ad, at the 'comp' (or good visual) stage. Show it to a dozen or so friendly customers.

Ask them: 'Which ad is most likely to cause you to contact the advertiser/buy the product? Which ad is the least likely?' When all three ads are subsequently run, such tests often show a strong correlation with sales leads received by each. Moreover, such tests allow your customers to troubleshoot your ads – such as for technical or health and safety errors in the photos.

Prove it for yourself. A test you'll love to apply is this: give your ad to your most articulate customer. Say, 'there's a terrible mistake in this ad. Can you spot it?'

I guarantee he will. He'll crow over your picture showing a lathe operator with long hair, or a building site with ladders not lashed to the scaffolding. Or your reference to a client who (yesterday) went horribly bankrupt. It's all welcome news to you . . .

Try this Awful Customer Test. It will rarely fail you.

16

SIX COSTLY MISTAKES YOU CAN AVOID WHEN PLANNING YOUR AD CAMPAIGN

1. *Failing to test the journal.*
One easy (but often neglected) way to test the journal is to run the same ad in all of them but code the response device differently. (You do have a response device, don't you?) This is commonplace with mail order (you quote Dept A, B etc in your address), but you can also do it in, say, retailing, where you want the customer to walk in.

In this case, your ad in Paper A offers a free gift, if customers bring the coded ad in or mention the ad; however, Paper B offers a price cut, if customers bring the coded ad in. Test the journal which pulled best, by running the ad there again, with a different offer. If this journal still pulls, you can place your future ads there with confidence.

You may even find that the traditionally despised 'free' weekly outpulls the local paid-for newspaper. (But keep testing . . . journals often change their profile and circulation over a period.)

2. *Failing to regard every ad as a direct response ad.*
With the exception of advertising run primarily to satisfy

legal requirements, all advertising is run with the hope that the reader or audience will do something as a result.

Even 'corporate awareness' advertising which intends to reinforce or reshape the market's attitudes towards an organisation or issue, expects readers to change their behaviour, in a way advantageous to the advertiser. Or why bother to advertise?

So monitor your ads – is anyone out there listening? On a small budget, the easiest way is to incorporate a response device. If a coupon or free literature offer is not appropriate, at least invite people to call a special number to hear a recorded message. Then you can count the calls made.

This approach drives in all-comers, then a step-sale can qualify them. For example, the first recorded message can conclude with a different telephone number which serious prospects can call to do business with you.

When Mobil campaigned against government curbs in the US, it ran whole page corporate ads in national newspapers. But it made sure to monitor them – it simply offered free reprints of the ads. One series alone pulled 11,000 requests – convincing Mobil its views had plenty of public support.

3. *Failing to specify position*
– and leaving it to the journal to run where *they* want it. The best place in the newspaper (to reach a broad spectrum audience) is close to the front, on a right hand page, above the fold, opposite the television programmes or the astrology section.

Second best, is in or opposite the news section – unless you are appealing to business readers, women or sports fans, in which case their section is obviously best.

Your *worst* position is probably the much-touted 'special supplement', particularly beloved of big local (and national) dailies, Chamber of Commerce journals and many trade magazines. You will simply be advertising to your competition.

Usually, these are simply 'ad get' features, too specialist for the general reader, too general for the specialist, and read by neither. Disbelieve this? Test it for yourself with a small coded ad which has pulled well for you elsewhere. Or seek editorial inclusion of your company in the supplement, on its own merits. If the journal insists you take an ad as a 'quid pro quo', decline – quality journals with a worthwhile readership do not need to blackmail you in this way.

4. *Failing to create a campaign.*
Design a uniform 'family' identity into every ad: repeat logo, layout, 'signature' (your unchanging slogan which sums up your unique benefit). Then every ad – regardless of size – builds on its predecessor. Otherwise, you have to build credibility from scratch every time.

And run your campaign month after month. Ads designed to sell off the page work best (if at all) on their first insertion – subsequent insertions usually show a steady drop in response. But those designed to drive people into retail outlets (a two-step sell) often need some time to bite.

5. *Failing to prepare for the response.*
A thousand sales leads arriving on your desk at once are just expensive waste paper – unless your organisation is geared to cope. Elsewhere in this book are suggested plans for handling response effectively.

6. *Failing to plan a 'backsell'.*
Someone who has happily bought from you once is your hottest prospect for further sales. Particularly if you invite them to buy a new product just after they have enjoyed your last one. If you have nothing left to sell them, you are throwing away opportunities. Plan a multi-step 'backsell' programme that develops a continuing relationship with your customers. Soon you may be lucky enough to need only 'maintenance' promotions – those which simply top up the 15 per cent of customers per annum who change their address.

```
┌─────────────────────────┐
│                         │
│        PART 2           │
│                         │
└─────────────────────────┘
```

Make your direct marketing more profitable

17

THE TEN MISTAKES IN DIRECT RESPONSE BEGINNERS MOST OFTEN MAKE – AND HOW TO AVOID THEM

I'm indebted to direct-marketing maestro John Fraser-Robinson for these cautionary pointers:

1. Not including a letter . . . it's the first thing readers read.

2. Not repeating the offer on the reply device . . . it's also one of the first things they read.

3. Not using a specialist supplier to design your direct response package . . . dm is as different from conventional advertising as PR is from journalism.

4. Not testing . . . seemingly trivial differences in package concept can double or treble your profit. Every time you mail, you can test something.

5. Not using long copy . . . the more you write, the more the serious prospect assumes you've something good to say. But it had better be *professionally* written and laid out.

6. Not using a PS . . . it's the second most read part of the letter.

7. Not asking for the order . . . spell out exactly what they must do to get the benefits, and repeat it over and over.

8. Not using a specially designed letter . . . your standard company letterhead wastes the most valuable space, the top, with the least interesting item – your name.

9. Not laying a path for the eye . . . deliberate devices of phrase and design should lead the reader through the copy.

10. Failing to set clear targets . . . you should know your break-even per cent and desired cost-per-reply precisely for each mailout.

Amen.

18

HOW TO DESIGN A DIRECT MAIL PACKAGE FOR RESPONSE

If you want to walk on water, you'd better learn to swim, was my partner's acerbic comment after I had run my first marketing seminar. (It wasn't really that bad, was it? Yes.) Eight years and 240 workshops then passed.

Some 4000 delegates later, here are just some of the Great Truths the Guild has learned – painfully and expensively – about business-to-business direct mail in recruiting delegates. (A word to our competitors: it's no use trying to steal our Great Truths. They are fully protected by decoy statements.)

Today, 1500 folk each year pay us up to £200 for a one-day workshop on public relations, advertising, direct marketing or copywriting – most of them invited by mail. Our competitors charge up to £400 per day. (They have to charge a lot, because I suspect some don't have too many repeat customers.) Our margins are lower – so we must make our marketing work very hard.

To get one delegate into the room we must spend around £105 on direct mail. Add hotel costs, travel, accommodation, equipment hire and admin, and we gasp with joy if we net 15 per cent. That's before tax. And before write-offs: for example, the seminar topics that flopped. The 'sure fire' lists that tested well but mysteriously misfired on roll-out. Do you have these problems too?

Delegates who gasp at our apparent income 'for just one day's work', having counted the house, reckon not with the cost of getting them there. In fact, to attract 1500 delegates each year, we must invest around £150,000 in direct marketing. Not a lot by *Readers Digest* standards, but big enough to lose your shirt if you get it wrong. The following is what we have learned, the hard way, by getting it wrong – initially at least, and learning thereby.

1. *Plain Janes can win . . .*

The designer shuddered, as he lifted one corner of our best-pulling brochure. 'It's not exactly tacky,' he said, 'but . . .' The reproach was audible. So he redesigned it. As an oil painting. Four colours. Heavy art paper. Fit to win an award, it was.

It bombed. My theory is that glitz cuts no ice. Direct mail which is too blessed by design has no nasty 'hooks' to arrest the eye or guide the pen. Readers are reluctant to mar its perfection, to scribble and tear at the booking form. It glides, much admired, into the bin.

Our next mailshot was just a letter, thoughtfully written but hastily produced on the office typewriter, and full of spelling mistakes (corrected in blue pen). Plus a typed 'self mailer'-type booking form. No brochure. No 'design'. It outpulled our control package by 325 per cent.

Design in direct response ads exists solely as a vehicle to make the sale. It is not there to 'create a mood', get the reader to exclaim 'how clever', or build your corporate image.

Sometimes the best direct response ads have the corporate imagemakers chewing their bow ties in despair. They are homely, 'down market', even downright crude – in the best sense of the term, implying simple, honest and unpretentious.

Some of the most expensive items have been sold solely by a letter, typed on a manual typewriter, and 'instant printed' cheaply in just two colours.

For example, several of our delegates have confirmed they made five-figure sales – by sending customers and prospects a photocopy of a 'new product' press release. This outpulled response from their glossy brochures, because its modest format bypassed sales resistance and, moreover, gave recipients a privileged 'preview' of an item others would not see until magazines printed it, weeks hence.

2. *Photos must support copy and convey benefits . . .*
Powerful four-colour photos grab attention, but will only work in direct response if they support the benefit – and the benefit is spelled out in the copy. The photo should show a person enjoying the product's benefits, and not merely show the product.

They will *not* work, if they merely stop the reader. Their objective is to get the reader to read *and* respond.

3. *Copy is king in direct response letters . . .*
and the letter is far more important than the brochure. It can often stand alone. In split tests, a letter and response device alone have often pulled just as well as a more expensive package that includes a brochure.

And, if there is one rule in direct mail on which most agree, it is that long copy outpulls short copy (usually).

107

The more copy the reader reads, the more likely they are to buy. The more expensive (or unlikely) the offer, the more copy you need to do the job.

One US travel agent sold $5000 speciality holidays – in the Arctic – solely by means of a seven-page letter.

This breaks the rule of brevity, which applies to billboards and press releases. In direct response letters, if what you want to say can be said in one page, take two pages, and say it all twice – but in different words. This does not mean being longwinded: your style must be tight, lean and powerful, or you lose readers. But repetition of key benefits, describing the same sunset from many different angles, works.

4. *Every component must sell . . .*
Put the entire sales message on *every* item in the mailing package.

That means, the coupon. The reply envelope. The letter. The price list. As well as on the brochure. You can't predict which item the prospect will read first, or how the items will be separated later.

The acid test is: will every item, if spotted casually by a third party in, say, someone's in-tray, cause them to stop and read it? And give them enough information on its own to order from you?

In particular, the response device is the place to summarise the benefits, the absence of risk, the free gift or discount, the need to respond *now* or be forever disconsolate. It should be a mini-ad all by itself. Because here is where the prospect will hover indecisively, pen in hand. It's where he needs the greatest encouragement to proceed.

5. *Good design in direct response is not achieved by whim . . .*

it's a precision-engineered machine. To work, it must follow proven rules. First, gain *attention* with your headline (and/or photo). Immediately, offer your key *benefit*. Follow with subordinate benefits. Give *proof* of your benefits, with testimonials, independent reports, etc. Show why the prospect runs no risk, by detailing your *guarantee*. Ask for the *order*, explaining how easy it is to place the order. Tell them what they'll gain by ordering before the cut off date, or what they'll lose by delaying.

Remember too the order in which readers read, and position each stage of your selling sequence in the reading order. (More on this in the section on writing ads.) For example, the postscript in a letter (or last paragraph in a direct response ad) is often the second part read, immediately after the headline (or the photo caption). Here is where you repeat your strongest benefit. Or give a reason to reply now. Or repeat the premium offer. Or all three. Don't be afraid to have two PS's.

For the same reason, a sales letter should have odd numbers of pages: three or five or seven. Why? The last page is the strongest selling page, in terms of the 'call to action'. Thrust it in front of the reader. Make it always a right-hand page, i.e. don't ask the reader to run over. (So if yours is a two-page letter, expand it to three pages. You should more than pay for the extra paper by extra orders.)

Add variety to your letter design by varying the paragraph width. The eye is drawn into and down a page where each successive paragraph is five or ten characters slimmer than the one above, like a reverse pyramid.

Varying the widths also lets you highlight separate copy elements, such as a case study, testimonial or list of benefits.

And break paragraphs and sentences over each page, to tempt the reader to turn over.

All that said . . . you can overdo adherence to the Great Rules of Direct Mail.

The first direct mail letter I ever wrote to promote the Guild's seminars couldn't fail. It contained underlinings, marginal graffiti, three different paragraph widths, a testimonial in a Johnson box, a photo of myself (wearing the Honest Grey pinstripe), a guarantee and two PS's. Plus bullet points reinforced with yellow highlighting (now there's a good idea!).

It failed. As one delegate commented afterwards, it contained every direct mail device known to the marketing profession. Which is why it failed. *Because I mailed it to the marketing profession.*

Could it be that the business market (if not the consumer market) is a lot more sophisticated today than in the sixties?

6. *Use action colours . . .*

The bright primary colours red, orange, yellow, green, blue offend corporate ad specialists, because they are strident. Which is why they work. (Brown, buff, silver, mustard yellow or beige print colours convey quality, but they do not excite. Do not use them, if you want response.) Paper colour in a direct mail letter should be white or cream, with black or blue print, if you want response. Because these combinations are the easiest to read.

That said, there's evidence that printing your reply

card or other action device on a pastel coloured stock, say, green or blue, will lift response. Because it calls attention to itself in the package.

7. *Every design feature must sell* . . .
For example, you will certainly create attention if the top of your letter is covered in dirty fingerprints printed in a second colour! But they had better lead directly into your key benefit.

For example, 'These aren't the only marks burglars leave behind' – for a security product. 'How often has the repairman had his fingers on your photocopier?' – for an office equipment firm.

Graffiti grab the reader too. I mean hand-scribbled notes, arrows, circles, diagrams . . . printed in a second colour. Yellow highlighting over your key points also lifts response. Underlinings work, particularly if done by hand in a second colour.

But because these devices are so powerful, each must reinforce a benefit and be used with discretion. Over-doing them leads to clutter.

8. *A direct mail letter should be typed* . . .
just like your office correspondence. *Not* typeset. *Not* justified at the right margin, even if your word processor makes this easy.

Indent heavily the start of each paragraph. And leave wide margins left and right, at top and bottom, of your text.

9. *The more items in a direct mail package, often the more responsive it is* . . .
(and the more expensive). Start with a full, busy pack-

111

Dear Reader,

If you think this offer is "too good to be true" - then I don't blame you. It's hard to believe anyone can afford to give you a free trial without any obligation.

Frankly, we only do it for one reason. Our experience proves that it's far and away the least expensive way of recruiting new members. Especially people who are looking for genuine good value, and are rightly suspicious of "amazing" offers. People like you, in fact.

Only by having a free trial can you prove to yourself that we <u>do</u> offer the lowest prices, and that you really can save at least £50 a year - and probably a great deal more - with Comp-U-Card.

So why say "No" when you could say "Maybe"? Why not return your Free Trial Voucher now?

John Fullmer,
President of Marketing
Comp-U-Card International Inc.

'Lift letters' should summarise the key benefits and urge action. They are best signed by a separate individual who can add his or her 'endorsement'.

age: use the response from this as your control. Then take elements out one by one until the profitability falls. This is better than starting with a lean package and building up, because you can test precisely the relative value of each component.

10. *A direct mail package should involve the reader . . .*
For reasons best known to psychiatrists, response increases if readers have to play with the package in some simple way. Like sticking on a stamp saying 'Yes'.

One proven involvement ploy is the 'lift letter', sometimes called the 'publisher's letter'. It's usually titled 'Do not open this unless you have decided not to respond.' This ensures it is opened first. It carries an 'independent' personal request to you to reconsider the offer, and packs in all the sales points again.

Consider writing your lift letter (like the response device) *first*. If original in its conception, it will be one of the most persuasive elements in the pack . . . particularly if it contains some genuinely independent element, like a testimonial from a named customer. Or a laboratory report. Or a quote from a magazine report on you . . .

And try printing your lift letter on a different paper stock, perhaps a coloured stock. Or a ragged-edged 'hand made' paper bearing a simulated handwritten note. Or consider the 'garbage memo', an inter-office memo apparently written in haste and stuffed into the envelope at the last moment. I love this one:

'Al, be sure to tell them we've cut 50 per cent off our list price for computer labels if they order by end of the month! Bet they won't believe us! How can we convince them? Bill'

Designers will scream at your inserting the 'garbage' memo into their beautiful package, but what do designers know about direct mail?

A (costly) variation of the lift letter is a separate tiny envelope affixed to the outside of the outer envelope. It reads 'Please do not open this until you have read the letter inside'. Of course, it is opened first . . . and gives powerful reasons why the prospect should open (rather than toss away unread) the main package.

11. *Envelope teasers can kill*
I believe everyone who says that envelope teaser messages lift reponse. In consumer mailings, that is. Because the average UK household receives only 3.4 direct mail items per month, an enticing envelope on the door mat demands attention. Even junk mail-haters will open it.

But my office in-tray averages twelve teaser envelopes *per day*. How about yours? On a busy morning, I – or m., secretary – used to junk unopened all the teaser envelopes, particularly those with irresistible offers: 'You have already won a prize! See inside . . .' Because they were so obviously junk mail and the 'prize' was certain to be junk too. (Later, we learned to collect them for our 'ideas file', but that's another story.)

Our own tests with envelopes suggest that cute or clever teasers depress response in business-to-business mailings and that overwhelmingly the most effective is a plain white C4 window envelope (expensive, so it can't be junk mail.) Or an important-looking plain legal-sized manilla, marked 'For the Personal Attention of:'

The exception to this is where an envelope overprinting can hint at a relevant benefit ('Inside – a five pound note!' Inside, sure enough, there *is* a five pound note, but of obsolete design – and shredded. The respondent can claim a real fiver, when he agrees to a sales call.)

Alternatively, an envelope message can be genuinely helpful. For example, prepare a rubber stamp 'The information you requested is enclosed.' Use it when mailing back details which respondents have specifically requested. This ensures your package doesn't get binned in error, along with the junk mail.

19

HOW TO ADD CREDIBILITY TO YOUR OFFER

Guarantees, endorsements, independent tests, all are invaluable credibility devices, as we've seen in the section on writing ads. But your direct mail copy needs even more credibility. Because it is fighting the six Great Obstacles: Disinterest, Censorship, Boredom, Delay, Suspicion, and Inertia. Here are some ways to overcome these obstacles and bridge the credibility gap:

1. *It helps to tell the truth*
– most especially, when it hurts. Showing warts and all is a good policy. Admitting to a weakness or a (non-significant) difficulty, strengthens the rest of your statement.

'Now, I'll admit this product is probably not for you, if you have less than 10,000 sq foot of warehouse space';

'This cookware uses a special ceramic finish to achieve its lovely burnished colours, so please don't use it in your microwave!'

2. *Get somebody else to 'write' your letter.*
Your secretary? 'Believe me, I sit here all day answering customers' phone calls and I *know* how good this product is. Customers love to tell me! Why, only yesterday a buyer from a top firm called me and said . . .'

This person, although hardly impartial, imports extra credibility. It's why newsletter promoters drop in an extra 'lift letter' from the publisher, to strongarm the sale. Incredibly, it works.

3. *Even better is the Triangle.*
This is where you get the reader on your side, by referring to a third person not present and gently making a joke at their expense.

'Quickly, before our accountant gets back from holiday, grab this offer now!'

'My partner will skin me when he finds out, but . . . I'm marking all prices down by 10% for 30 days.'

I particularly love this one:

'WILL THEIR WIVES EVER FORGIVE ME? Developing this product for you has meant a 60-hour, 7-day a week schedule for my best design people. Gladly, they've sacrificed their evenings, even their weekends, so you can have the best. Now . . . it's ready. Please try it . . . and tell me it was worth it. Please . . . Before their wives find me. Hiding here in this closet'.

Perhaps this is as close as you should get to making a joke in a direct response ad. You want a sympathetic smile, not a horse laugh.

The Triangle is an amusing attention-getter. It attempts to enlist the reader's sympathy – and a smile.

4. *Testimonials don't have to be from big names.* Your spouse may do fine. 'I attest that Mr Robinson has put blood, sweat and tears into writing this book for you, and now I'd like my kitchen table back. Thank you. Signed Mrs Robinson.'

5. *Don't be stingy on your money back guarantee.* Be specific and brave. And make it the key benefit of your letter or ad. For example, if you are promising a 100 per cent return on investment within three months, from a £100 newsletter, say: 'If you have not more than paid for your subscription within three months of following this newsletter's advice, we will refund every penny you have paid. And you keep the copies you have received.'

If your advice could be worth £5000 over twelve months, state it boldly in the headline: 'Your £5000 guarantee. If over the next twelve months our newsletter fails to show you practical, proven ways to make at least £5000 profit, write and tell us so. We will immediately refund your membership fee without question.'

Apt variations of this will work well with products too. 'Take three months to prove it for yourself. If you're not convinced that the MiniMarvel is the best little thing ever to happen to your factory floors, we'll take it away and you'll owe us nothing.'

One US refuse collection firm boasted 'Satisfaction or double your garbage back.'

The few refunds you have to make under a bold guarantee will be more than made up by the extra orders your show of confidence brings in.

State a long guarantee period. It actually reduces rather than heightens the risk of money back demands. All but the most dissatisfied customers will long have forgotten the terms of your guarantee, by the time it nears expiry. Dare you make yours a lifetime guarantee? The way that Parker Pen does?

One company (not Parker) did this, the *wrong* way. Whenever the customer brought in a product for free repair, their invariable response was 'Sorry, our lifetime guarantee covers the lifetime of the product. And as you can see, this product is *dead*.'

That company is no longer in business.

20

WHY SELFMAILERS OFFER YOU LOW COST, HIGH RESPONSE . . . FOR 'LEAD GET' CAMPAIGNS

The self-mailer is an all-in-one device that does away with the need for an envelope, or for any separate components at all. The simplest example is a postcard. Indeed, the lowly postcard can be a very cheap, fast mailer to announce a sale, a bargain offer, a new store, new product line, or just company news of value to the customer (like your change of address or telephone number).

More complicated self-mailers may consist of a letter, mini-brochure, and reply device ingeniously printed and folded from one sheet of card or paper. They are still low-cost because the printing and folding takes place in one run, and there are no multiple elements to incur insertion charges.

Self-mailers work best for low price items, which invite impulse purchase. Or for step sales that, first, solicit an enquiry which is answered by a more expensive letter and brochure package, or by a telephone call or sales visit.

If you seek a high-volume response, rather than a repeated attack on just a few selected prospect companies, self-mailers can be far more cost-effective than the conventional three-step multi-mail campaign. (This is the practice of telephoning first to establish the name of the decision-maker, writing him a personalised letter, then following up by telephone to seek an appointment.) Their percentage response can be unusually high, because they often have a high 'pass along' readership. Particularly if you print a 'routing box': 'Please pass to Works Manager . . . Works Engineer . . . Maintenance Engineer . . . etc'.

You don't need to target by name. In this rare case, job title will do almost as well. Where named individuals are hard to come by, you can often attack compiled lists of companies by job title alone – normally the least effective type of mailing – and still get a profitable response.

The outer surfaces of self-mailers are designed for very fast reading, like mini-posters. You should pack your key benefit into big headlines on front *and* back. Then whichever way it falls in the mail tray, it will sell (and hopefully, stop a passerby to fish it out).

Print them in extra-large and/or coloured stock to attract attention. One design is mailed out, so that the prospect's name is visible on the outside; to respond, the prospect completes the information requested and folds the card the other way so that the advertiser's return address appears.

Self-mailers are so inexpensive, you can productively mail a different one each month (use different messages and colours to avoid boredom setting in).

Motivity is a company which claims it can 'do everything' that involves hand labour. Its regular mailshots are irresistibly readable. Because they list the entertaining and unlikely contracts it has fulfilled, like 'affixing 30,000 labels irremovably to record sleeves.' Then 'removing said labels.'

But Motivity could do even better. By printing a different 'unlikely contract' every month on a self-mailer postcard, Motivity would have a superb – and very low cost – continuity lead-getting campaign.

21

HOW TO WRITE COMPELLING
DIRECT MAIL COPY

Direct mail is a very personal communication. Consider, if someone stopped you and asked 'I'm going into a meeting in thirty seconds. Why should I recommend my company buys your product?' you wouldn't start talking about your team of highly qualified design engineers, or your company's fifty year pedigree, or your ergonomic efficiency.

You'd gasp, 'It cuts downtime on your trucks by at least 15 per cent, and will pay for itself in nine months. After that you get a big saving every year that goes straight on to your bottom line, and increases your profits.'

Now your prospect is happy. In fact, your copy exists to sell – not products or features – but happiness. So everything discussed in the section on writing ads applies to direct mail copy, only more so. And with the wonderful addition, peculiar to direct mail, that you can genuinely . . .

1. *Personalise your headline or salutation.*
The simplest way to personalise a headline is to use the

word 'you'. If you can also insert the prospect's own name (and spell it right), you are certain to get attention. Laser printing makes this possible now. Only . . . every example I've seen looks so unconvincing that I'm sure it would depress response!

And I suspect that any extra orders gained can be wiped out by the horrendous cost. Like desktop publishing, this dubious advance is still in its steam age.

It is also unreliably dependent on computers. I have framed one laser-printed letter from a direct mail company (no less), addressed to me as Chairman of the Marketing Guild. It begins 'Dear Mr M.Guild . . .'

Often you'll get nearly as good a response as a personalised letter, with a generic salutation: 'Dear accountant . . . marketing professional . . . customer . . .' But avoid 'Dear friend'. The prospect is not sure he wants to be your friend. You have yet to convince him.

But I like the idea from one of my delegates. He advises you start: 'Good morning, Mr Jones!'

An ingenious way to 'personalise' a letter was exploited by a firm which sold tours to Ireland. It targeted all the McClure families in the US who had above average incomes. The letter began 'On behalf of the Ancient and Royal Clan McClure and the men, women and children of Ireland, it gives me great pleasure to invite you and your family to attend the historic Grand Reunion of the McClures in Ireland.'

Every year, this company sends two chartered Boeing 707s across the Atlantic, filled with 1200 clan members attending their historic reunion. Can you imagine the scene at Shannon Airport when the tannoy asks 'Will Mr McClure please go to the Information Desk'?

When all the McClures in America are used up, it will probably turn to the McClurgs, and so on!

Seriously, is your database large enough that you can mail all the 'Mr Smiths' and 'Mr Williams' and 'Mr Jones' with a 'personalised' letter in this way? (Um, that's an idea. We have over one hundred Smiths on our own database . . .)

2. *How design can help.*
Design can emphasise your personalised headline: 'Mechanical engineers! Cut project time by 15 per cent . . .' For example, you can set this in bold. Or in simulated handwriting. Or use a second colour. Blue is most often used, because it allows you a blue signature at the end without going to the expense of three colours.

But a powerful headline – whether personalised or not – can consist merely of a Johnson Box: that is, a statement set in a heavy box above the salutation. You may not need the expense of studio work. You can type a Johnson Box on the word processor, using asterisks for the frame. (An American delegate told me that the phrase Johnson Box came from the US and originally referred to an athlete's truss. Which is why my innocent advice to him, to put his testimonials in a Johnson Box, reduced him to helpless hysteria . . .)

3. *Dare you get intimate?*
Insurance companies have long understood the value of personalising their direct mail, even to intimate lengths.

If urging a present client to take out a new policy, they'll write a letter which shows specifically how much benefit the reader (Mr John Brown) could gain (£50,000) in just a few years time (eight years) if, at his present age

(42) he increased his present premium (£15 per month) by a trifling sum (£5). And wouldn't his wife (Mrs Brown) and two children (Jim and Jane) enjoy the added security too?

Of course, the insurance company can do this because it has these details on computer. You too probably have more information on your customers than you know. (See later for how you can exploit this with Micro-Mailings.)

But the more intimate you get, the more hate mail you'll get back. People don't always like being told 'I know you'. Particularly if you obviously don't.

Prince Charles, whose annual income exceeds £1 million, apparently received a direct mail letter which began 'Dear Mr Windsor, Wouldn't your neighbours at Buckingham Gate be surprised if next month you and your family proudly drew up to your home in a brand new Ford Sierra?'

Wouldn't they indeed?

22

HOW TO ACQUIRE BETTER MAILING LISTS AT LOWER COST

'I would to God thou and I knew where a commodity of good names were to be bought'
Henry IV, Part I.

Familiar wisdom says that a mediocre package mailed to a good list will pull response, but even the best possible package will fail if the list is wrong. I had painful reason to confirm that in my apprentice days, when promoting a textbook on photography. A list broker mentioned to me a list of 'trade photo names' which, he suggested, were all 'professional photographers'.

Some £1500 and nil response later, the broker casually revealed that they were not pro photographers at all, but just ordinary folk who had sent in their holiday snapshots for processing!

The lessons I learned were that (a) list selection is critical, and (b) some 'list brokers' are blissfully ignorant of their craft and will sell any plausible rubbish to a gullible punter.

(At present, anyone in Britain or the US can trade as a list broker, without experience. And the prospect of mandatory accreditation for list brokers has gotten no further, after 20 years' discussion.)

So be warned! Here are some tips, to help you avoid the worst predators in the list jungle:

1. *The cheapest lists you can buy.*
These are 'compiled' lists. They have been put together from publicly available sources: directories, electoral rolls, membership lists, and the like. Usually, they are very outdated, given that some 15 per cent of businesses, 30 per cent of jobholders and 25 per cent of households move each year.

Most are available only by company name and address, occasionally telephone number as well. (Sometimes you are offered a limited selection of job holders' names too, but their currency should be checked. We found that names in one of the most popular business directories presently sold in Britain were at least 25 per cent out of date just one month after the directories were published.)

Usually, compiled names are sold outright, i.e. they become your property and you can re-use them as you wish. Which raises the question: why should anyone claiming to have a good list wish to sell it to you outright, if they could rent it to you time and again and make lots more money? Answer: probably because they know the list is worthless, and you would never come back to them for a second rental!

Compiled lists are also inherently poor-responders, even if totally up to date. One reason is that mailings addressed by job title only are too often discarded in the mailroom or secretary's wastebin. Moreover, at least 40 per cent of those addressed to named individuals will also be wasted – *because that is the percentage of people who virtually never respond to direct mail, regardless of the offer.* (In fact, serious moves are afoot to compile a central database of proven *non*-responders. These names will be rented out at premium prices, simply so direct mailers can remove them from the other lists they rent!)

Even if you could buy outright a totally up-to-date compiled list, it would date quickly – and become almost useless within two years, unless you regularly clean off the 'gone aways'. List maintenance can be a full time job.

However, sometimes you have nothing else but compiled lists to work with. At least they save you time in finding directories and typing your own labels. And to be fair, they do sometimes work. Mailings made to companies by job title may pull leads, particularly if you use low-cost mailings such as self-mailers which incorporate a wide and strong appeal. (See the chapter on self-mailers.)

Cheaper even than buying such lists is to compile your own from directories. If yours is a local business, don't neglect the electoral roll, available in main libraries and Council offices. You can then choose the districts you want – affluent, rural, urban, whatever. List compilers call this demographic selection. Given the provisos above, it works.

If the typist's fingers rebel, you can rent labels taken from the 1.4 million company names listed in Yellow Pages. Apply to the Business Database: 01–567 7300. It has the merit of being continually updated.

A very cheap way to reach affluent individuals, is to ask the Company Registrar of a successful corporation to divulge the names and addresses of its shareholders. Under the Companies Act 1967, section 52(2), it is obliged to, if asked. These names may be virtually free.

Choose companies which have just declared big dividends. (The Company Secretary can, and must, tell you where to find the Company Registrar.)

One way you might succeed with a compiled list is to mail carefully chosen companies with many mailshots per company, each addressed to a different job title. Around 20 per cent of companies employ some 80 per cent of the staff in any given industry or profession. It could be these few companies are the ones you most want. Hit them often, and at every level.

One way to do this, without risking offence, is to do '*series mailings*'. You plan a series of mailshots, each building on the one before. The first is a teaser, the next reveals your offer and asks for the order. The next says something else about your offer and asks for the order. The next gives them an urgent reason to respond now (a 'cut off') and asks for the order. And so on.

The secret is to (a) pre-print all your mailings so that each can be released at short intervals, perhaps just a week apart. And (b) make each mailing entertainingly different. You want an expectant smile from your reader, as he opens the package. Not an angry letter to 'take me off your list'.

Dealer incentive schemes often use series mailings, usually staggered at longer intervals. One promised a holiday in Japan for the winning dealer. So each month, dealers received a letter printed with the Japanese sun emblem. Only each month . . . the sun dipped lower on the page ('time is running out . . .').

Between letters, dealers received souvenirs of Japan . . . like a paper fan, chopsticks, a miniature bottle of saki. Finally, each received a postcard from Japan, signed by the resort manager, saying how much he and his staff were looking forward to entertaining the winning dealer.

Multiple hits on one firm won't save you money up-front (forget the hopeful ploy of inserting several envelopes in one outer and asking the mailroom to sort each into the right pigeon hole by job title!). Rather, you profit because (a) the eventual order in a series mailing is likely to be substantial, and (b) once you have one order from the company you can use this 'testimonial' in selling to other individuals or departments in the company.

2. *A better idea for very low cost mailings is portmanteau mailings.*

Several non-competing suppliers with the same prospects in common insert their material into one package, and split the mailing costs.

The drawback is that response per item is usually much diluted, but the low mailing price may outweigh this. Several companies offer such 'portmanteau' deals commercially. They gang together several firms in a regular package to, for example, doctors, accountants, librarians.

The Gas and Electricity Boards offer portmanteau mailshots, letting your leaflet ride along with their bills. On a local level, of course, you could ask newsagents to slip your material into newspapers they deliver.

Or you can make your own approach to non-competing firms, to arrange for two or three of you to send portmanteau mailouts to the same market.

3. *An even better way is the hitchhiker.*

You ask a non-competing firm serving your market – and probably already mailing it – to mail your material to

133

their customer and enquiry list. This often works amazingly well, because the list has already proven responsive. *Make sure you also gain an endorsement from the list supplier.* (His satisfied customers trust him, the way your's trust you. So if he recommends you, they'll transfer their trust to you.)

You do not pay him a fee for this. Instead, you code your insert, so that you pay a flat sum for every order or enquiry you receive from this source. This cuts your risk, and also gives him a chance to make more money than by simply renting a list to you.

Of course, he may insist that a secure third party handle the mailing, so that you cannot simply steal his list. You'll want this protection too, if you ever offer to mail another firm's material to *your* list. (If you do, be sure to seed your list with decoys. These are fictitious names which bear your home address or those of friends, so you can track who's mailing your list with what, and spot any abuse of your list rental agreement.)

4. *Gain valuable lists entirely free . . .*
from a non-competing firm which mails your market. If your 'house' lists are comparable in nature, do a straight swap of equal quantities. But check the quality of their list first, by exchanging samples.

A quite big (10,000) exchange of 'marketing directors' I did on trust with one publisher proved a near-disaster because, on examining his labels, I found a good half were of 'sales executives'. When challenged, he said 'they're the same thing, old boy'. Curiously, some professional list brokers know no better either!

But be aware that, if you do swap, your list can now quite innocently migrate by degrees into the hands of your direct competitor. Company A swaps or sells it, as part of its own list, to Company B which does likewise, and so on . . . Perhaps this doesn't matter if, by that time, the origin of each name is lost. Putting in decoys will help you track your list as it travels.

A safer approach is to exchange labels with the other party upon request, both of you keeping track of how many 'contras' you've exchanged. But agree *not* to incorporate each other's names in your database or pass on each other's lists to a third party. Trust and common-sense can make such deals surprisingly productive. I use them continually for seminar promotion.

5. *Try 'merge and purge' . . . but cautiously.*
What's merge and purge? Suppose you have a 'house' list of your own customers and enquirers . . .

Your best *rented* lists are those which already contain plenty of your house names. The more they contain, the closer the list is to your own market profile! But of course, you don't want to mail the same people twice or (worse) simultaneously. It makes you look inefficient. And they complain . . .

So you obtain the rented lists on computer tapes, and a bureau merges them into one list (along with yours, if it's on computer tape). It then purges out the duplicate names. This can save 15 per cent or more on your total direct mail costs.

However, you need to process a lot of names, so that the average 15 per cent or so saving on duplicated names (which you now *don't* mail) exceeds the cost of the merge and purge process. And sometimes it's impractical. Many small business-to-business lists are not available on computer tape. But for numbers in excess of 20,000 it can pay you well, by eliminating waste. Of course, ensure your list broker negotiates a 'net names' deal, whereby you don't pay list suppliers for the names they duplicated.

You must be very cautious about merge and purge, and here's why . . . The Guild rents a dozen or more lists at a time, many not computerised. So duplicated names are inevitable. People complained. And we used to worry about this. One day, we paid a bureau to de-duplicate three big rented lists which happened to be available on tape. After bureau costs, we found ourselves a few hundred pounds better off in postage saved – and several thousand pounds down. Because the mailing flopped.

Yet the same lists and package had worked well six months previously. Explanation? No, it wasn't brochure or list fatigue (the declining results you can get from mailing the same thing to the same people too often).

We found it was the duplicate names who had been booking our events!

If they appeared on several different lists of prior responders, they were by definition 'high responders'.

Of course, it had made sense for us to hit these hot names several times, even with the same package. The vagaries of rebate mail had probably staggered the arrival of our duplicate packages over a period, ensuring that the prospect gained several intermittent 'opportunities to see' our offer.

De-duplicating these names had destroyed our mailing.

Now when I ask Guild delegates 'how many of you have received more than two of our brochures in the last three months?' and every hand shoots up, I'm in no doubt that (in business-to-business mailing, at least, and using small lists) duplicated names are no bad thing.

6. *Save money on 'nixies'*
These are packages undeliverable by the postman. At £300 per 1000 upwards, nixies returned from an outdated list can eat up your profits. So send your nixies back to the list supplier for a rebate.

(Most good list suppliers will guarantee their names are at least 95 per cent up-to-date: an 'undeliverable' rate much worse than this gives you ammunition to talk down their invoice.)

Don't forget to stamp a message on the back of the envelopes: 'If undelivered, return to . . .' And do the same on mailouts to your own list. Why on the back? The envelope looks less like junk mail, and is more likely to be opened.

7. *How to double the response from your mailing.*
This is a dark secret, whispered only between direct mail professionals. Carry out the usual merge and purge – but tell the bureau to retain the duplicated names in a separate file.

These are your most valuable prospects. If they appear on more than one list, they have proven their responsiveness to mail offers!

Re-mail these 'hot' names later, perhaps with a different offer. They will be far more responsive than the whole list. This extra mailing is very low cost indeed, because your merge and purge has saved you the equivalent cost of mailing them the first time. Let me explain:

Merge and purge three lists, each 10,000 names: 30,000
Save (say) 15 per cent duplication on each list (total
names saved: 30 per cent): 9,000
Thus, net names mailed: 21,000
Net cost saved (9000 @ £300 per 1000): £2700
Remail 9000 duplicates @ £300 per 1000: £2700
Thus: Mailing cost of second mailing (£2700 saved less
£2700 spent) equals zero
Add: Cost merge/purge @ £20 per 1000: £180
Pay list suppliers pro rata for re-use of names @ £75 per
£1000: £675
Total cost of second mailing is thus (cost of merge/purge
payment to list suppliers): £855 or £95 per 1000 inclusive.

As a result, you have gained at below one third the
normal cost (£95 compared with £300) a second mailing
which, although smaller than the first, should be far
more responsive. The end result is that you gain perhaps
twice the profit return – with only an 8 per cent increase
on your budget.

Note that you *must* tell the list suppliers you are re-
using their names, and pay them accordingly.

The reason this 'secret' is whispered about, is first,
because it is enormously effective (sometimes it pays to
throw away the unduplicated names, and mail *only* the
duplicates). Second, retaining duplicate names in this
way gives dishonest mailers a tempting way to steal a
list. Because a duplicated name is unlikely to be a decoy.
Why? It appears on lists from different suppliers.

However, your computer bureau – and possibly mailing house – will know you've cheated, and the word will
get around. The list suppliers will probably sue, for
infringement of your 'one time only' rental agreement.

And besides, there are foolproof ways to know if someone tries to steal your list, even in this way. You simply make sure that your decoys are, not only on your own list, but also on every list your customer is likely to rent!

How to do this? Enquire for information about their products or services, well before you need their lists. Use an assumed name, one you can identify later, and a different one for each external list. Add this name to your own mailing list too. That way, if they rent your list, and merge it with their own list and others, then purge out the duplicates, they'll find the same name both on their rented lists and your list. So it gets purged as a duplicate.

If they subsequently steal these duplicate names from your list (thinking they can't be your decoys) and they remail them without paying you again (or the other list suppliers), you'll know it – and have the evidence to sue them. Or at least, to avoid them in future.

Is it worth the hassle? I have for many years inserted my own decoy names in both my own list and every external list I regularly exchange with publishers and seminar organisers. And I assume they have their own decoys in my list. The UK seminar business is a relatively small one. We know each other.

When one well-known organiser of PR seminars tried to steal names in this way from two of us, we all knew about it, and none of us will now trade with him. List protection *is* worth it!

Of course, if you have purchased the lists outright, they're yours to merge and purge and do with as you wish. You pay no further rental costs, on either the duplicated names or the others.

8. *Make your lists pull harder.*
Remember that the response behaviour of individuals (as opposed to groups) varies greatly at different times. Whereas 'demographics' attempts to describe buying behaviour in terms of where people live, 'psychographics' describes buying behaviour in terms of people's attitudes and lifestyles.

For example, for certain products, lists with the salutation 'Ms' supplied by the person typically outpull lists styled 'Mrs'.

But there's another term you may not have heard of: 'synchrographics'. It describes buying behaviour in terms of the changes which occur in people's lives. New appointees, new brides, buyers of a new car or new home or new factory, new parents – all undergo major temporary changes in their buying patterns. All are suddenly in the market for goods and services to fit out their new lifestyle or enhance their new acquisition.

If you want to increase the pulling power of your list, target people in this way by 'synchrographics' rather than conventional groupings. How? Keep an eagle eye open for changes in their situation, virtually any change – and mail a highly personalised letter. (Or tip off your sales force accordingly.)

9. *Rent 'responsive' lists this way.*
These are lists of people who have proven they respond to direct mail. If you can still make an acceptable profit, it literally does not matter what you pay for them per thousand. In 1989, £85–£120 per 1000 is a reasonable rate for proven responders. But I happily pay £300 per 1000 for one list which is wonderfully responsive.

By comparison, a compiled list of 'cold' (i.e. non

responsive) names selling outright for just £50 per 1000 sounds good. (After all, I can use it after the initial purchase as much as I want.) But it is actually appalling value! Because 40 per cent of those names will never respond to direct mail, and some 30 per cent are 'gone aways' before I've mailed them. The actual cost for the part of the list which is both responsive to direct mail and current is at least £210 per 1000.

To find responsive lists, contact an ethical list broker. A competent broker can reveal to you a diversity of available lists from a great many sources, some you never suspected.

Many, of course, will derive from publishers who keep scrupulously clean reader lists, categorised by geographical region, job title, type of business and purchasing patterns. Volumes of similar lists, categorised by lifestyle or purchase data, can also be had for consumer marketing.

Once, we laboriously rented lists from a dozen or more publishers direct. Now I do it with one telephone call to a broker. It costs us no more, because the broker takes his commission from the list supplier. And we gain, free, a lot of good advice about new lists on the market.

Only do ensure your 'list broker' knows a Mosaic from an Acorn. Most don't.

10. *Specify the responsive lists you really want.*
And you just might get them. The key words to ask a list broker are Frequency (how often do these people buy?), Currency (when was the list last cleaned of gone aways?), Recency (how recently have they bought?) and Purchase value.

Invariably, the most frequent, current and recent lists

– and the larger volume purchasers – are the hottest for your mailing. Some list suppliers term these their 'hot' list and charge a premium. It's usually worth paying.

Remail an enquiry list until the cost outweighs the potential profit. But that may not be until the sixth or seventh mailing. A good list can be used over and over, without exhausting it. That's because, in our own tests, as many as 25 per cent of people simply never receive any given mailshot. Someone else has binned it. Repeat mailings increase the chances of their receiving at least one.

It's also because there exist 'junk mail junkies' who will respond to virtually *any* mail offer in their interest area. You can't mail these people too often.

Some direct mail pros recommend mailing a different package to your 'hot' list at least once per month. This is 'relationship marketing'. It appears to mean that people buy most happily from their friends, and a friend calling in each month with a welcome message gets more business.

With these special people, you'd target them individually, refer to past purchases, remind them of their interest areas . . . and make your mailshot as much like a 'me to you' personal newsletter as possible. Even if you have to individually word process and sign each one.

In fact, micro-segmentation of your list this way can pay dividends. Even if you keep your list on file cards, you can use micro-segmentation. How? Simply categorise each customer in three segments: Major purchaser, Medium purchaser, and Small purchaser. Next, segment them again in terms of Recent Purchaser (last six months), Not-so-recent (six to twelve months), and Old purchaser (over twelve months).

It's up to you where you set the goalposts. Because the

point of this process is that you now have a matrix, with nine cells. Each of your customers fits into one of them. It now becomes child's play to send a different letter to each customer, referring to how much they spent with you last time and how long it's been since they ordered.

It's child's play, because you need only draft nine different letters. You send them out in batches; first, all recent big purchasers, then all not-so-recent big purchasers, and so on. Result: each customer feels special. You have correctly identified them, and acknowledged them as individuals. Response increases. And you can do this just with a manual typewriter, a photocopier and a card file.

When you *do* know your customers personally in this way (as opposed to thrusting intimacy upon total strangers), extreme personalisation is well worth the trouble.

Eg:	£10,000+	£5000+	£1000+	
0–6 MONTHS	**1.**	**2.**	**3.**	
6–12 MONTHS	**2.**	**4.**	**5.**	
OVER 12 MONTHS	**3.**	**5.**	**6.**	Recency of purchase

Purchase value

How to micro-segment your own mailing list. Figures indicate priority of customer. The higher the priority, the more frequent the mailing.

11. *What to do if still you just can't find a list for your market.*
Incidentally, this is your free bonus section . . . if not
completely satisfied that it will resolve your problem,
return it to me unused and keep your problem. (Forgive
me . . .)

There certainly can be times when no list exists, such
as when you are marketing a totally new concept or
targeting a very specialist market. Bald left-handed
hairdressers in South Wales may flourish in their hundreds. But, if you have a product just for them, no list
broker can help you find them. More realistically, many
firms seek out purchasers of equipment or services who
are not definable by job title. Or by reading matter. Or by
any other formal criteria.

For example, if you're selling all-purpose industrial
plastics containers, major purchase decisions can be
made by anyone – from the works manager to the company secretary. Who do you mail?

In this case, you have – patiently and sometimes
expensively – to build your own list. You need a step
programme. The first step is to ask your prospects to
declare themselves. Place an ad, targeted specifically at
your buyers.

'Do *you* buy plastics containers? Discover how you can
save 25 per cent or more *plus* improve use of your warehouse space by up to 30 per cent! Call this Hotline number
now (24 hours) for a FREE Information Pack, revealing 15
proven ways you can trim your handling costs . . .'

Then you follow the sequence for step programmes
detailed elsewhere in this book. (Incidentally, this plan
works. I spent four years selling plastics containers.)

23

HOW TO PREDICT YOUR MAILING RESPONSE

Some textbooks tell you to research the market for a new product you intend to market by direct response advertising or direct mail by 'dry testing', asking people's opinions. 'Would you buy this product at this price?' But people like to please. They tend to say Yes.

Our delegates were virtually unanimous, in questionnaires they returned to us, that they would book a one-day 'intensive' follow-on to our PR seminar. No set agenda. Just syndicate work. Each syndicate would address a real-life problem presented by one of the delegates. Heartened, we set the event up and mailed them all and not one of those 4000 stalwarts booked. Zero response. (Is this a record?)

Moral: the only direct-mail test that's worth a damn is one that (at some stage) asks people for money.

Conventional wisdom has it that you never gamble your shirt by mailing to an entire list. You test 5000 first. If that works you double up to 10,000, then 20,000 and so on. So your risk is always controlled. Legends abound of the direct marketing experts who were so sure of a list, they mailed it all – only to find it was the wrong list.

Once, a big publisher (a normally reputable company) offered me 30,000 'mail-responsive sales directors'. I mailed them all and got about three replies. It later transpired, their list was actually of miscellaneous 'promotional names' they intended selling their magazines to. Not sales directors at all. And certainly, not responsive.

The fault was mine. I had broken the basic rule: never believe one word that a list supplier says. You *have* to test. And test small.

A test of just 5000 is adequate to test the pulling power of a list. To test more subtle points – like headline, premium offer, or response device – conventional wisdom says, you need at least 20,000 names. Trouble is, the UK has a relatively small population. Some lists are just not big enough to yield you statistically reliable test results. Even if you mail the total list.

But suppose you have three different small lists to test, plus three different packages?

You can still try micro-testing. It does not give you the precision which will allow you to predict results from a large rollout. But that's not your problem – you've got nowhere to roll. It does let you test both lists and packages simultaneously, at minimum risk and cost, and guides you on which lists/packages pulled best/worst, and which to repeat (or drop).

Suppose Package A contains a letter, brochure and your standard offer; package B is the same as package A, only you offer a big discount; package C is the same as package A, only instead of the discount you offer a free premium item, say, a calculator.

You have three lists each containing 10,000 names (the concept works on even smaller lists, but less reliably).

Ideally, List A is your 'control' list, one you have used before and know what response it pulled.

Split your mailing as shown in the diagram. Your lists are split in half, each half receives a different package. You code the reply device in every case, according to the list it was sent to and the type of package.

Provided your offer is of a kind to pull at least a 0.3 per cent average on your control list (i.e. you should receive around 30 per 10,000, for meaningful analysis) you can easily determine (a) which package pulls best over all the lists, and (b) which list pulls best over all the packages. You then repeat-mail the best package to the entire list (or lists) which proved profitable.

Direct mail testing is as near a precise science as the marketing profession knows, provided you do it scientifically. Vary one single major element at a time, and

Responses gained

LIST PACKAGE	A (CONTROL)	B	C	TOTAL	PACKAGE RATING
A (CONTROL)	30	12	40	82	No. 2
B	10	5	6	21	No. 3
C	42	6	58	104	No. 1
TOTAL	82	21	104	207	
LIST RATING	No. 2	No. 3	No. 1		

Micro-testing for small lists. Three packages and three lists tested simultaneously. (Outright winners are package C and list C, which outpulled control package A and list A.)

147

compare results against your control package. For example, a typical 'concept' test might compare personalised (laser printed or word processed) mailings with standard printed mailings.

Be aware that, in mailings smaller than 100,000 it is usually not worth testing minor items like colour of envelope, first versus second class mail, postage stamp versus post imprint. But in large consumer mailings, where a 0.1 per cent difference can mean thousands of pounds, as many as thirty subtle variations and combinations are often tested.

When testing, also note that product demand is sometimes seasonal, and that certain seasons can depress (or lift) sales, even in business-to-business markets.

Tradition has it that the 'best' months for direct mail are, in priority order, January, February, August, September, October, November . . . but these schedules are virtually meaningless. Every market, offer and mailshot is different. Carry out your own tests and note the seasonal variations over time, or else your predictive results will be badly skewed.

24

USE THE YCWTA FORMULA IN
DIRECT RESPONSE

YCWTA stands for You Can't Win Them All. It means a winning direct response idea is certain to offend someone somewhere. After all, your intention is to be provocative, to grab the reader's attention. Not everyone likes being grabbed.

One of the most successful mailings ever done by Scientific American magazine was packaged in a brown envelope with the teaser message: 'Caution – inside you will find material of an arousing nature.' They meant, of course, lush full colour photographs of wildlife. Disappointed clergymen and teachers wrote outraged letters. A few subscriptions were lost. But sales soared.

I once sent a personal letter to every newly appointed marketing executive announced in the trade press, congratulating them, and inviting them to a seminar. (New appointees – like new brides – are a prime list for direct mail. It's the new-budget, new-broom syndrome.)

I received two furious telephone calls: one from a lady who had held her present job for many years, and was *not* (she told me acidly) a new appointee; and one from a lady who had just that morning been offered a new job, was terrified the news was already public knowledge, and thought I was a black magician. (I still don't know how either happened.)

I was sunk in gloom – until a few days later, when I counted our amazingly high returns from this mailing.

Apply the YCWTA formula – tempered with common sense – when testing unconventional direct response ideas or even controversial media, like telex and e-mail. If they work, fantastic. If not, what have you lost? Remember it took Thomas Edison 8000-plus attempts to invent a light bulb that worked. Now he's a household name. But had he given up, under the lash of consumer disdain, would you or I have heard of him?

25

SIX WAYS TO MAKE YOUR DIRECT RESPONSE CAMPAIGN WORK HARDER

Direct response ads sell. Other forms of advertising create or sustain awareness, as a precondition for selling. Direct response ads are *not* awareness ads. *Unless they work at once, in a tangible and profitable way, they have failed.*

It is often quite difficult to tell if an awareness ad has worked at all. This difficulty is compounded by companies which (unbelievable but true) fail to build in any device to monitor if anyone's out there. So they travel blind, firing golden arrows into the void.

But direct response ads are the toughest of all to create. Because there is no way to fudge results. Either the ad or direct mailshot brought in sales leads or cash, or it didn't.

To make your direct response ad (or mailshot) work, recognise that it must squarely face major barriers. Other forms of advertising never face these barriers, because they never go to war. But you must learn to confront, and master, them:

1. *Disinterest*
Ads will be acted on, only by those who have a pre-existing interest. Hence the importance of targeting the

right list, i.e. those who will want your offer and can afford it. The best mail piece in the world will fail, sent to the wrong people. But even a poor piece may succeed, mailed to the right list.

Note that direct response ads cannot reach everyone. I've said before that at least 45 per cent of any compiled group of people (for example grouped by profession or region, rather than by prior evidence of their responsiveness to direct mail) will throw away your mail piece unread or even unopened. They do not buy by direct mail. Don't waste money addressing them. Prune them out. *Direct mail will not normally educate a cold prospect*. It's more profitable to preach to the (direct mail) converted.

2. *Censorship*

Remember, up to 25 per cent of your mailing pieces will never reach your intended person. Mailrooms, secretaries and spouses will discard them; even the Post Office sometimes fails to deliver. If you get, say, a profitable 5 per cent response to your mailing, and receive 50 orders from 1000 pieces mailed, you can be sure you would have got an even better response, perhaps 67 orders (6.7 per cent response) if all your letters had arrived.

This is one reason you can repeat an identical mailing to a good list and often get as good a response again. It takes several mailings to 'use up' a good list, and the responsiveness will revive, if you leave the list alone for a few months. It is also the reason you must use every ethical device possible, to get your piece to the right person – and opened by them.

Putting 'Personal and Confidential' on a letter which is blatantly not so, is not ethical; moreover, it does not work. Better is to run a headline of ten words or more across the envelope, which promises a benefit. (Benefit copy on envelopes in household delivery is said to out-pull teaser copy four to one. Mere teaser messages on envelopes – at least in business-to-business mail – can actually *depress* response.) The reader has to open the envelope to get the benefit. You have to pay to print the post indicia anyway, so the message rides free.

3. *Boredom*

Your best list is your prior customer list. They trust you. Your profitable future lies in building a relationship with them. 'Relationship marketing' implies many, many mail shots – perhaps one per month or more.

But even customers will get bored by your repeated mailings, if they all seem alike. So vary them in insignificant ways: change the envelope size or colour, change the print colour of the letter, overstamp the letter and brochure with a 'Final Opportunity!' type message. These devices do not depress the pulling power of a successful package, but *will* help people read your message more than once.

4. *Delay*

Your next best list is your enquirers. These have already told you they are definitely interested.

Next to existing customers, they have the highest conversion-to-sale ratio. But their interest wanes with time. Bounce back an acknowledgment of their interest at once, and keep soliciting them. This way, conversion ratios of one-in-three or better are commonplace. Yet our own research suggests that, across all industries, 45 per cent of all enquiries (sales leads) are never followed up at all, still less followed up in 24 hours.

5. *Suspicion*
Customers aside, a recipient of your ad does not know you. Yet you are asking for money (or some commitment). Why should he trust you? Prove your bona fides, over and over.

Use testimonials, endorsements, independent research, before-and-after photos, names, addresses, telephone numbers they can call.

A Post Office Box number is instant death in direct response ads. It implies you are ashamed of your address, or are lurking in a motel just one step ahead of the fraud squad. Offer a money-back guarantee, if the goods are returned in 28 days. By law, you have to, anyway. So make a virtue out of necessity, and emphasise it. If you accept payment by credit card, say you will credit their account if they return the goods. In practice, fewer than 3 per cent of customers will demand a refund, if your product or service performs.

6. *Inertia*
The prospect is about to order . . . and something distracts them. They put down their pen. No sales rep is present to steer them back to the order pad. The sale is lost. *For every one order you receive, at least one is lost because of last-minute procrastination or interruption.* Or the prospect could not find a pen (stamp, envelope, chequebook, whatever).

This is another reason why good lists work time and again. Your latest shot reminds the almost-customer, and this time they find their pen. And they order. So make it easy for the prospect to say Yes.

Enclose a pre-paid reply envelope, several reply cards (both loose and integral to the brochure), put their name and address on the reply card or coupon so all they need do is tick a box or stick on a 'Yes!' sticker.

Include a Freephone or LinkLine tollfree telephone number (and put it on *all* parts of your mailing – you never know which the prospect will read first).

If your product or service costs more than £100, chances of prospects buying it 'off the page' fall sharply. So let them respond in easy stages: try a step sale, as illustrated elsewhere in this book.

For example, advertise to get enquiries, and service the enquiries hard: a telephone call to qualify them (and cull out the timewasters), a full brochure-letter package and a follow-up call. This sequence will cost at least £15. So step sales are rarely profitable, if the order value is less than £100. The cost of servicing enquirers is too high.

And be aware, the easier you make it for a prospect to respond *without* sending money up-front (and the more prominently you use the magic word Free in your headline), the higher your returns and bad debts. Timewasters and cranks find direct response ads and direct mail a happy hunting ground.

If you haven't tried a direct mail campaign before, you may get very depressed by the number of reply paid envelopes returned to you, at your expense and presumably by adults, which are stuffed with rubbish. Once, we removed the reply paid element, so a respondent had to put a postage stamp on the reply envelope. People *still* sent us rubbish complete with a postage stamp at their own expense!

The good news is that a large number of nuisance returns at the start – and they're always the first to arrive

– invariably heralds a good response later. I don't know why this is, either.

Don't give away the store. If you get more than 5 per cent returns or bad debts, reconsider. But normally these 'painless purchase' devices drive in more than enough extra business to compensate for the nuisance returns.

Recognise these barriers to your direct mail success, and you can overcome them.

26

21 MAIL ORDER IDEAS YOU CAN STEAL . . .
TO BOOST YOUR RESPONSE

The simplest way to get new ideas for your direct mail package is to get yourself onto as many mail lists as possible. Not just your competitors', but those of businesses quite different from your own.

Everyone who receives direct mail reacts like a consumer, whether they are sitting in their office or kitchen. Cross fertilisation of ideas between consumer and business-to-business advertising works. Because we are all consumers. Meanwhile, why not steal these ideas?

1.   Use an ordinary brown paper bag. Insert your mailing piece, staple, stamp and mail. But tie it in sensibly with your headline: 'Good things come in strange wrappers'; 'Your product solution is in the bag', etc.

2.   Simulate a bank statement, exactly like the real thing – window envelope, no overprinting. Inside, your message starts 'Discover ten ways to add big credits to your bank statement quickly', 'Build your bank deposits faster with new xxxx'.

3. Overprint the envelope: 'Your cheque is enclosed' –
and include a simulated cheque made out personally to
the individual or company for whatever sum you wish.
Your letter explains 'You could bank this sum and more
today – and every day – when you stock xxxx products'.
And offer to honour the cheque for cash or credit with
their first order.

4. A motor trader printed a letter on a windscreen
washcloth: 'We'll put a polish on your car free, when you
drop in to inspect our new range.' They enticed in
dozens of amused motorists – and while the forecourt
staff were polishing their cars, they could offer a shrewd
guess at the trade-in values.

5. 'Your snaps are enclosed'. Ever need to get your
message to the buyer, un-intercepted by the secretary?
One of our consultancy clients printed up a yellow envelope, just like those used by the photolabs. On top were
what appeared to be unposed family snapshots, each
with a cartoon caption. They led to photos of products
with the captions 'Introducing our new family.' Finally,
was a reply paid card showing a further family snapshot
and an invitation to caption it – and receive product
details.

It was his most successful mailer ever. The secret of
such cheeky but effective mailers, of course, is to
sidestep offence with humour and creativity.

6. Try a genuinely handwritten PS. In small numbers,
it's feasible. And the impact is enormous. The most
persuasive direct mail letter I ever received was painstakingly written in capitals with a biro on a plain piece of

paper. From a local courier business, thanking us for our business. We've used them ever since.

7. Attach a 10p coin to the letter, with the suggestion they use it to call you. (They might, if you choose your list wisely.) Or staple an old £1 note to the letter. Or a foreign banknote. Or enclose a pack of shredded currency. (If the bank won't sell it to you, try buying foreign bank notes of negligible value from collectors, and shredding the notes yourself). Your message reads:

'This is the cash you're wasting every moment of the day, by not using . . .'

Now comes the crunch: 'If you're not the person I should be writing to, please pass this letter (and £1 note) to the person in charge of . . . Thank you!' Offer to redeem the banknote (or its simulation) for a real credit against their first order.

8. Try 'wallplanner bingo'. In December, you mail a free wallplanner to prospects – a maintenance wallplanner to engineers, a distribution planner for warehouses, etc. Each wallplanner has a prominent number.

Every month, mail the prospect a letter with a new offer. The PS in the letter contains a simple quiz, answerable by reading the letter. Answers yield a four-digit number. Prospects then check if that number is theirs. If it is, they phone in for a gift. Result: your sales letters – and wallplanners – receive prominent attention throughout the year.

9. Another jokey ploy for gaining entry with any sort of office product is the office plant award.

In January, you mail a small packaged rubber plant

with instructions. As it grows during the year, mailings refer to it. Plants are measured at year-end by the sales rep – an obvious excuse for a sales call – and the largest plants are awarded a prize. Silly, but fun. And very inexpensive.

10. Use a postcard – particularly a giant one – with a strong dated offer on the reverse, plus a tollfree LinkLine number. Ideal for announcing sales or special offers. Or if you're new in town, buy an aerial photo of your town. Print this as a giant postcard, with your store arrowed and a headline 'Come down and see us some time . . .' Particularly if you can put a coloured dot on *their* premises to show how close they are to you.

11. Try a telexshot. You might be lucky and they'll work for you. They cost as little as 50p each from a bureau, and work best to announce last minute irresistible offers. Use them before they're banned.

12. Likewise, you could try a facsimile shot. It can cost as little as 13p to fax an A4 letter across London, during the weekend. Bureaux exist which can multiple-fax thousands of your messages automatically. And faxes are 'urgent'. They get read. (That is, until too many people complain about finding their fax paper rolls emptied on Monday morning and the floor strewn with junk mail. At their expense.)

13. Simulate a telemessage or old-style telegram. Direct mail veterans disdain this device, because it has been around so long. Yet the odd yellow envelope still gets opened first – along with envelopes that look impressively official, such as legal-sized manilla.

14. Include a sample. Firms have sent actual roof tiles. Carpet tiles. Industrial absorbent cloths. Or you could give a voucher, good for a free 30-day trial. You'll find most customers will want to keep it. This is the 'puppy dog' sales technique. Or give the first business service free. This is the 'guilt' technique. Yes, some prospects will abuse it, but it may still prove very profitable – by driving in volumes of new customers.

15. Give a bulk imprinted envelope a first-class personal touch. Affix cancelled postage stamps as well (buy in bulk from a stamp dealer). Cancelled foreign stamps add extra interest, if relevant to your offer.

In a now-legendary mailing, a department store featuring international goods stuck on stamps from many different countries and over-printed the envelope: 'We've gone around the world for you . . .'

16. Stamp 'DO NOT OPEN' on the outer envelope. Inside is another envelope: 'Do not open . . . unless you want to save £2000 on your office supplies in twelve months.' Inside that is *another* envelope: 'Do not open unless you have the authority to purchase office supplies worth £20,000 or more this year'. Inside that is a still smaller envelope: 'Do not open unless you have the vision to seize an opportunity you may never have again!' Expensive, but irresistible . . . and profitable, for some products.

17. Put a yellow sticker on the envelope: 'Review sample. Submitted to . . . Your help is needed and will be greatly appreciated. Kindly examine the contents of this mailing – then, if you wish, please send your criticisms or comments to: . . .' Not only will you get comments (some of them useful), but also you will get attention – and orders. (I am indebted to Shell Alpert for this one.)

18. Mail a bulky or crinkly package, that obviously has a mysterious enclosure. Like a Christmas stocking, it begs to be opened. In tests, bulky enclosures like pen-and-pad mailings drew double the response of flat enclosures of equal perceived value, like stress indicators.

19. Overwhelm them . . . if your potential payoff is very high. A bank delivered just 1000 mailshots in three teaser stages. Each stage cost £10–£25. First was a real house brick (a small one): 'We're as solid as this brick'. Next stage was a real diamond (industrial quality): 'We're as bright as this diamond'. Last stage was a real plug-in desk telephone: 'We're as close as this telephone. Plug it in. Call us now.'

It worked, for the big-ticket investment schemes they were selling. So they say.

Another firm selling design engineering techniques to automotive manufacturers mailed just fifty boxes. Each contained a 28-page brochure and a five-minute cassette – plus a portable stereo cassette player to play it on. The cassette had a recorded personal message from the firm's chief designer. Each shot cost around £30. They only needed one sale, to pay for the promotion. It worked. They say.

20. Write the ultimate direct mail letter, one on one. Study a handful of prospect companies very closely.

Discover their turnover, number of staff, latest product launches or business projects, trends in their market (complete with accurate numbers on market size, growth, etc.) – the same painstaking homework you'd want to do when first meeting a major potential customer face to face.

Find out by a telephone call the name of the person you need to write to, their job title, if possible something about them (the firm they last worked for, the job they were last promoted from). Weave all that highly specific information into your letter:

'With your sales approaching £12.23 million in fiscal 1989, your company could add £145,000 to its profits this year if you simply shaved 1 per cent off the distribution costs from your Maidstone and Brent depots. If you could add just another 1 per cent to your 16 per cent penetration of the £77 million UK market, your present sales would increase to £13 million . . . that's a very creditable £104,000 in sales for each of the 125 staff you employ, and well above your industry average. We have prepared a free report exclusively for you, Mr Jones, explaining how Smithy & Co can achieve these objectives in fifteen weeks. I will call your office in the next three days, to discuss when I can deliver this report to you . . .'

Such letters are hard work to research and write . . . and follow up. (Don't expect the prospect to call you back. You want him to wait expectantly for your call, with a reluctant smile of admiration for your cheek and hard work.) But all you need do is write a handful each month, and gain a good conversion-to-sale ratio on a big

An unusual legal-sized envelope and brochure get opened.

Brightly coloured 'telegram' style envelopes stand out in the In-tray.

ticket product. One thing I promise you from experience . . . most of those you write to *will* see you. They're dying to know what else you've found out about them!

21. Have you the nerve for this one? If all else has failed (and only then), write a letter like the one above to the big potential customer you've been courting. Fill it with nice things, compliment the company on its achievements, but gently point out how much better it could do if only it let you put your ideas into practice. Title the letter 'An Open Letter to xxx Ltd.'

Get your solicitor to vet it. Why? Because your next step is to buy a page in the prospect's biggest trade paper – and you *publish this letter* as an advertisement. At worst, you'll receive a cold letter from the company concerned (so what? You weren't going to get their business anyway.) Plus, expect to pick up some editorial comment – and a lot of admiring trade gossip. Better still, expect a few telephone calls from other big fish who admire your chutzpah and invite you to meet them. At best, you might even get the business you went after in the first place.

PART 3

Strategies to gain extra business

27

BUDGETING A SALES LEAD GENERATION PROGRAMME

Any programme will contain so many variables specific to your market and product and objectives, that proposing a 'model budget' is clearly risky. However, the following are two sample budgets for programmes promoting the sale of a mobile telephone product in 1988. One programme uses print media, the other uses direct mail.

Plan A: Coupon advertisement
Full page in A4 sales management magazine, black and white, right hand facing editorial matter, coupon at bottom right. Ad offers a free informational audio cassette.

Initial test ad:

Cost of space:	£2000
Design and artwork:	£500
Total for ad:	£2500

Valid leads generated:	86
Cost per lead:	£29

Add audio cassette @ 37p   £31.50

Conversions to sale (15%):   13
Cost of sale
(excl. direct sales costs):   £216

   Whether a cost of sale of £216 is acceptable on a product price of £1500, before direct selling costs, obviously
depends on the supplier's margin.
   Test ads are always the costliest. This cost of sale
would drop – and net profits increase – during repeated
insertions of the ad, assuming response remained stable,
as (a) space bookings would attract volume insertion
rates, and (b) design and art costs would be amortized
across the series.

Plan B: Direct mail

Test mailing
Four-page A4 letter, printed two-colours. Plus DL-sized
four-colour six-page product brochure. Reply paid card.
In DL-sized window envelope, overprinted with envelope teaser message. Mailed to rented list of 5000 named
sales managers. The package offers a free personal
organiser when they accept a 'test drive' of a mobile
phone.

Origination:
Design, art and copy: £1000
Plates, separations and setup: £500

Production:
Letter @ £50 per 1000:   £250
Brochure @ £42 per 1000:   £210

BUDGETING A SALES LEAD GENERATION PROGRAMME

Reply card @ £12 per 1000:	£60
Outer envelope @ £17 per 1000:	£85
Insertion: £25 per 1000:	£125
List rental @ £85 per 1000:	£425
Rebate postage @ 11.05p each	£552.50
Total (excl. origination):	£1707.50
Cost per 1000:	£341.50
Valid leads generated (3.4%):	170
Cost per lead	£10.04
Add cost of premium @ £5:	£15.04
Conversion to sale: (20%)	34
Cost of sale	
(excl. direct sales cost)	£75.20

This is obviously a far more acceptable cost of sale. Origination costs have been excluded in the total for this test mailing, as they are disproportionately large in relation to the rest of the budget and would artificially inflate the cost of sale figures to £94. However, they should be added back in, when the campaign is 'rolled out' across the complete list.

28

HOW TO PROCESS SALES LEADS
FOR MORE PROFIT

New sales leads have as much shelf-life as fresh fish in your refrigerator. They start to go off within a few days. Literally so – in the direction of your competitors. Yet a study we commissioned suggests that 45 per cent of industrial sales leads are never followed up! Including ones that might have brought major sales.

Likewise, in consumer marketing and retailing, sales leads are constantly neglected. In fact, the problem is overwhelmingly more acute in retailing than it is in industrial marketing.

A survey showed that 68 per cent of shoppers, who had bought once from a department store but never bought again, had not gone back – and for one reason only. *Nobody had ever asked them to!* The store had been sitting on a gold mine of potential new sales, and declining to exploit it.

All they had to do was go to their first-time purchasers and say please come back! When did *you* last receive a postal or telephone invitation to return to a store?

I know, they don't have your address or telephone number . . . (*But why don't they?*)

Most organisations will perish in time, without a fresh supply of new business to top up the old. So why do we all (and marketing consultancies like mine can be the worst offenders) habitually throw that new business away?

Three proven arguments for neglecting sales leads
1.   The sales force can feel insulted at having new leads thrust at them, which they are supposed to work into their journey plan. They become bellicose. 'I know these fellows – they're all timewasters' or 'If there's any significant new business on my patch that I haven't already found myself, I must be incompetent. Are you accusing me of that?'

(These are actual protests I recall from a sales meeting I sat in on, when the new sales lead generation programme was presented to them the *wrong* way.)

2.   The 'creative' aspects of marketing tend to be associated with the front end, the generation of sales leads. It's *fun* to design ads and promotions, to meet the agency and approve media schedules.

No one pays much attention to those tatty sales leads, when – long after the creative buzz has died away – they flop through the door. Because no one has created a plan to handle them.

3.   It appears to demand a lot of resources to log, qualify, monitor, analyse and process sales leads efficiently. The average sales office invariably complains that it lacks these resources (or the budget to contract the job out).

Result: sales leads are forwarded en masse, often

unopened, to the regional sales managers or reps. They flip idly through them, note the interesting ones to follow up on their next journey cycle, and file the rest in a shoe box.

Is this an exaggeration? *The majority of Guild delegates attest that this is almost precisely what happens in their organisations!* They know it's wrong, but changing the system – one explained – would be like moving the pyramids single-handed.

Here is a suggested plan to bridge the all-important gap between receipt of the sales lead and the sales rep's appointment. Consider if it can be modified to suit your organisation. Several of my consultancy's clients use it and attest to its success.

1. *Desk qualify the leads the moment they arrive.*
Is this one merely a literature collector? Is it worth taking this lead further? A fork lift truck firm inundated with requests from students and academics may bin them – why subsidise the education industry? But an electronics design firm may cherish them, because these are tomorrow's buyers or influences-upon-the-sale.

Don't be too quick to discard requests from company librarians. They often act as information-routers, and ensure your brochure goes to a prospect you'd never otherwise locate.

2. *Log the leads by source.*
Are they from ads, direct mail, PR, exhibitions, product cards, whatever? Each lead should be traceable to its source, if you have coded the response vehicle in some way. (Don't worry that some leads arrive uncoded. They tend to balance out across the different sources, so you still get a fair picture.)

Ensure that the switchboard or other telephone handlers capture the source of the lead, by asking 'Where did you hear about us?' Many callers will not know, unprompted, so it helps to code your material additionally for telephone callers, with the name of a fictitious contact person (this is detailed elsewhere in this book.)

Don't forget to log the time waster leads by source just as rigorously as the valid ones. Why? Because at year end, you can easily determine that Literature Collectors Weekly (say) sends you largely useless leads, and you can delete them from your ad schedule and PR mailing list.

3. *Assign a unique log number to each valid lead.*
One way is to use a simple numerical sequence.

Many computers can generate these automatically, ensuring a unique number. Additionally, assign a prefix identifying the type of lead (PR = editorial; AD = print ad; CD = product card; EX = exhibition; and so on). After this comes the individual number for this lead, allocated in numerical sequence. Then, a suffix identifies the specific source (SHD = Storage Handling Distribution magazine; BAF = Bafflex 89 exhibition; etc.). Finally, you might have a code for the specific insertion.
Your log number might thus read:
AD/25789/SHD/128.

Any data management programme on a personal computer can now categorise your sales leads at year end by type and source, by running a simple 'select and sort' routine. This facilitates the more sophisticated analyses suggested below.

Another method suited to firms with many sales

regions is to base the unique log number on the enquirer's postcode. In the event that two or more respondents live in the same postcode area (possible if it's an industrial estate), you add a further suffix to differentiate them. Thus LU4 8DLA and LU4 8DLB. By this method, the postcode can serve as an identifying prospect code – an economical use of computer space.

It also enables leads to be allocated automatically to the relevant area rep. And it makes it simple to correlate orders received, perhaps months or years later, with the original source of the lead. Simply look at the postcode.

4. *Enter the leads on computer.*
Can there be any excuse for a company not maintaining at least a simple computer log of its prospects, when an Amstrad and data management package together now sells for under £400? A computer system makes it almost effortless to produce personalised mailshots, analyses and reports. Perhaps even more important, it imposes a discipline for the handling and follow-up of enquiries.

No time to work a computer? One option is to have a part-time operator come in frequently for a few hours, to enter and process your sales leads. In this way, the job won't succumb to more urgent chores.

In practice, if you have more than a few hundred customer records, you'd benefit from a far more powerful pc than an Amstrad. For example, the Guild's database is held on a Victor VPC personal computer with a forty megabyte hard disk, enabling us to store details of 34,000 members plus all their transactions, seminar bookings and purchases. Plus registrations per seminar, VAT and accounts files.

As a result, we can send personalised letters to, say, all

potential seminar attendees in pharmaceutical companies with the job title of Product Manager, living in North London – just by typing an eight-digit code. The computer does all the ensuing select, sort and report (letter) generation processes automatically. Plus every imaginable kind of analysis.

This computer cost us under £2000, plus a further £500 for a data management package. Low cost systems like it should prove suitable for all but the most sophisticated sales office. No, you *don't* need costly 'dedicated' sales lead packages!

A tip: it can be a mistake to 'economise' by putting unrelated files, like payroll and accounts, on your customer database system. Once the accountants get their hands on it, you'll find it's always mysteriously occupied – and your newborn sales lead programme will perish.

5. *Sort enquiries into passionate, hot and cool.*
A few will want a rep to call or a telephone call at once. Process as Priority – ensure someone phones them that same day to seek an appointment. These are your 'passionate' leads.

'Hot' leads are other worthwhile enquiries. Handle as below.

'Cool' leads are the type that insist 'literature only wanted at this stage.' You send them literature but log on the computer for telephone follow-up after a period.

6. *Acknowledge all valid sales leads immediately.*
If he posted it to you, the enquirer has already waited several days or weeks. (Some journals' 'bingo' card systems work slowly at peak times.) He has probably forgotten about you. The hot lead has cooled.

So enquirers should ideally be 'qualified' at once. Telephone them to establish their degree of interest, budget, urgency of request, product needs, type of industry and application, and so on. Enter this information on the computer. It can then be produced as a report to pass on to the rep, who is thus in a far better position to make the call than if handed an unqualified lead.

Whether your telesales team also makes an appointment on behalf of the rep will depend on your manner of selling. Some reps prefer to have the prospect 'warmed' by a telephone call, but to call themselves to make the appointment. It is also far easier to staff a telephone qualification post in your office than a telesales post i.e. someone who actively sells by telephone. To be effective, the latter requires a lot of training.

If it's impractical to telephone each lead, at least write back a personalised letter at once, saying 'Thank you for your enquiry . . .' Remind the prospect what he enquired about and *attach a copy of the ad or editorial item which prompted it*! This warms up the prospect again and avoids the response: 'When did I ever enquire about a left-handed flidget?'

Failing that, remind him in your letter where his enquiry came from ('Thank you for your reply to our ad in SHD . . .') and summarise again the product benefits. Tell the prospect *why* he enquired.

Say that the local dealer or rep will contact him in the next (three) days. (Obviously, it adds credibility to specify a period, if you can.)

7. *Enclose customised literature.*
This step is arguable. Some firms will reasonably say that, if the prospect is mailed all the information first, it

preempts the sales rep's chances of gaining an appointment. Other firms find that mailing *incomplete* information whets the prospect's appetite, but gives the sales rep a chance to hand deliver the full material.

This was the case with an electronics distributor who fielded literally hundreds of leads per week. A full catalogue posted to each would have been expensive. Yet enquirers wanted detailed technical information. His reps could not personally visit – or even telephone – every hot lead.

The answer was to 'bounce back' a personalised letter with a short-form catalogue (a two-page sheet specific to the enquiry) *plus* a reply card. This card asked myriad questions about the enquirer's application, budget, purchasing authority, etc. If *that* card came back, it was treated as a 'passionate' lead and telephoned at once.

This method of qualifying the enquiry is worth considering in an emergency if you have too many leads to follow up. It sorts the 'passionate' from the 'cool' enquirers, but is obviously less effective than telephone qualification.

If you do decide to send literature, it markedly enhances the rep's welcome if you customise the package to the enquiry. For example, insert testimonials or client lists or case studies specific to the enquirer's industry.

8. *Periodically analyse the leads.*
Sort by type of product, geographical area, type of industry, job title of respondent, likely order value, and so on – in relation to the source of the lead.

Over a period, each source and journal will reveal – not

only a different ratio between valid and useless leads – but also a different profile of respondent. This will prove priceless for your future media planning.

9. *Pass the qualified leads to the salesforce.*
Some firms insist that leads are sent first to the area manager, who can add his own comments before allocating them among the reps. However, this builds in further delay, which is why it's so important to have telephoned (or mailed) the prospect meanwhile.

10. *Correlate the orders received with the source of lead.*
This can be the trickiest step. It poses no problem with a short sales cycle or a small organisation or 'off the page' sales, where the prospect buys from your sales office direct by post or telephone. It becomes more difficult, the longer the sales cycle and the larger the sales force. Add the complication of sales through dealers and some firms will say flatly, it's impossible.

But it can be done, as I know from three of my consultancy's clients. Each follows a process somewhat like this:

Each lead is assigned a unique log number upon receipt. Even 'cold call' leads which the rep finds himself are given a separate number. This follows the lead all the way through to the order.

If an order document is received by the sales office without its log number, this is identified from the computer records and added, where possible. But the rep is notified and loses points in the sales commission scheme. Conversely, if the log number is correctly added on the order form, the rep gains points.

Obviously, this works only if all reps follow a standardised system of documentation. And if the value of the system is properly communicated to them. (Better identification of sales lead sources, means more and better sales leads in future, which means more commission for them.)

A similar approach should work even with dealers, if built into their incentive programme.

Some firms will protest that multiple and repeat orders are often placed by a small number of customers. Should every order have its own sales lead number? Obviously not, if the order arose during the regular journey cycle. A separate code for 'existing customer', assigned by the sales office, can identify these.

But a unique sales lead number should still be assigned in respect of 'new leads' received by the sales office, even if the organisation is already a customer. Why?

(a) It may reveal interest from a new individual or department, which the rep should be aware of.

(b) Analysis of the purchase behaviour of your repeat purchasers, by source of lead, can indicate where your top customers gain their product information. This should guide your allocation of budget towards, say, more money on PR or product cards or a specific category of media or whatever, to reach more of these prime prospects.

(c) If too many sales leads from existing customers come direct to the sales office, rather than via the reps, perhaps the sales manager should be asking his team a few questions? If they nearly missed those opportunities, what others are going begging?

11. *Determine cost per sale.*
One of the advantages of being able to tie up orders

received with the source of lead is that you can, over a period, derive priceless information. For example, the computer will readily break down sales by broad source of enquiry (PR, ads, product cards, etc.), and then by specific media. It can then reveal the average cost per sales lead, conversions-to-sale ratio, average order value and the average contribution to the cost of sale per order made by the sales lead generation programme.

You may find that, say, results from PR and product cards compare like this:

Product cards (averages):

Cost per sales lead: £6

Conversion-to-sale: 20 per cent

Unit order value: £250

Unit cost of sale (excluding direct sales costs): £30. Net: £220

PR (averages):

Cost per sales lead: £20

Conversion-to-sale: 33 per cent

Unit order value: £500

Unit cost of sale (excluding direct sales costs): £60. Net £440.

From this (admittedly very simplistic) example, it is readily apparent that product cards yield sales leads at low cost, and probably a large number of them. But their conversion to sale ratio and the average order value is relatively low.

Leads from editorial PR, however, cost more but their conversion to sale is higher, and they bring larger orders.

A comparison like this may not necessarily suggest that product cards or PR are better or worse than each other in the sales lead programme. They demonstrably have different roles and can support different objectives.

For example, experience suggests that an editorial PR programme based solely on customer case studies will probably yield far fewer leads than one based solely on new product releases. But case studies should yield responses giving a higher conversion to sale and higher average order value. (Because prospects know more precisely what they're enquiring about.) Conversely, leads from product cards may convert well for, say, hand pallet trucks up to a certain price range but be less effective in identifying purchasers of 'turnkey' systems for automated warehouse control. Which cost a lot more and take many steps to close the sale.

Having such information and value comparisons to hand can obviously be very powerful when arguing for greater budget allocations or a different split in budget. And their use in media planning for advertising or PR work is clear.

HOW TO PROCESS SALES LEADS IN CONSUMER MARKETS

Firms advertising to the consumer market have traditionally faced great problems in tracking the sales process, from the point where the consumer sees an ad all the way through to the purchase in-store. Of course, indirect methods of evaluation abound: market research among shoppers, recall figures for a given ad, consumer contests which ask shoppers to identify ad themes, and the like.

But increasingly, firms with consumer markets are exploring more direct methods of testing ads – and gaining 'leads'.

● One firm encloses a coupon in its ads. When mailed back, it brings a free sample of the product, plus a discount voucher which the shopper can redeem in-store. The firm can thus test response to the ad, and count redemptions. It can deduce a precise relationship between its ad spend, and the profit gained, *before* adding in the likely purchases of this product which a shopper – once introduced – may make in future.

Moreover, it builds its own database of shoppers who can be mailed periodic offers.

● Another company cherishes its returned warranty cards. When analysed, they reveal – not only masses of data about the lifestyle of its customers (which helps media planning) – but also opportunities to sell them other products. For example, a purchaser of video equipment who admits to an interest in stereo will be mailed Privileged Customer offers on stereo accessories.

Similar techniques can work even for individual retailers. How many keep a database of their customers, by item purchased, address, even birthdate?

Yet gaining this information is simple: merely hand customers a self-mailer type questionnaire with their change. They gain a small gift if they post (or bring) back the card. A gift is then 'reserved' for them. Of course, they have to come back to the store to claim their gift . . . whereupon you have another chance to sell them something.

After a time, a busy store will have created a large mailing list. Now it can post birthday cards to shoppers – and enclose a voucher for a modest gift they can redeem in-store. It can congratulate mothers on their off-spring's impending birthday – and suggest suitable gifts.

It can announce special offers, promotions, seasonal price cuts. It can remind them of Valentines Day and urge them to shop early for Christmas. It can tell DIY purchasers about a new gadget, or gardeners about a wheelbarrow offer.

Eventually, it will build a community of loyal repeat shoppers. At this stage, it launches a Customer Club and a shopper-get-shopper programme and a newsletter and . . . the possibilities are boundless.

These examples suggest that, both in business-to-business and consumer marketing, the principles of sales lead development are the same.

Capture the sales lead, qualify it, and systematically build a relationship with the customer that can bring you the most profitable sales of all: repeat business.

29

CATCH LOST CALLS – WIN MORE SALES

Probably more sales are lost because of bad telephone handling at the supplier end than . . . well, you name it. Yet an 'efficient telephone system' was barely rated in a new British Telecom survey of small firms. What had most impact on their image? Top came 'company's staff' (43 per cent), then 'premises' (17 per cent), but only 7 per cent cited 'telephone system'. But the 'most irritating factor' when these firms tried to *contact* a supplier – quoted by 31 per cent – was, yes, an 'inefficient' telephone switchboard.

Is yours foolproof? Ask a dozen friendly customers to test your switchboard – by calling it, disguised as confused prospects bearing hot sales leads. Issue them audit forms, to rate your switchboard's response time, helpfulness, professionalism, etc.

(And why not call your switchboard yourself – and ask for yourself? Count the rings before answering, and note the words and manner in which they tell you, that you're 'not available'. How would genuine callers react?) Then use the results to argue the case for better switchboard training.

APPENDIX

CHECK YOUR SUCCESS RATING . . .

against these 44 Ways to Improve Your Ad, Brochure or Direct Mail

We all know that successful ads – or any promotional message, for that matter – rarely result from a blinding stroke of genius. More likely, they are the accumulation of many small points of detail, the designer's experience of what has worked before – and what hasn't worked.

The following 44 guidelines summarise the key points of this book and provide a checklist of what works. Apply it to your next campaign – and see how it boosts your results.

The headline

1. Do you have a headline?

Amazingly, some ads don't. Yet it's where – after the picture – the eye first falls.

1a. Have you put a key benefit in the headline?

Otherwise, the reader has no reason to read on.

1b. Have you refrained from using your company name as *the* headline?

It can be an excellent idea to put your name in the headline *linked to a benefit*. Then the 80% of readers who read no further will at least take away some meaningful message. But as a headline alone, your name is your weakest message and is wasted in your strongest place. Your name belongs at the 'call to action' position – usually the bottom.

1c. Likewise, have you avoided using your product name as *the* headline?

Alone, it does not convey a benefit. But linked with a benefit, it can make a powerful direct headline.

1d. Does your headline directly state your proposition?

If the reader has to stop and think what it means, usually he won't bother. Research suggests that direct headlines pull several times more than indirect (or cute, or jokey) headlines.

1e. Do you stress 'you' not 'we'?

'You can now enjoy the perfect motor car' is stronger than 'We have perfected the motor car'. A lot of corporate ads in particular are 'we' rather than 'you'-orientated. They lose readers.

1f. Is your headline long enough?

Long headlines (within reason) work better than very short headlines, because you need adequate space to convey a benefit that stops the reader.

1g. Have you appealed to the emotions?

'Imagine how *you* could enjoy 10 per cent more profit' is stronger than 'Cut your inventory by 30 per cent'. The first addresses the right brain (emotions), the second addresses the left brain (logic). Both appeals are needed in a responsive ad, of course, but emotion makes a better headline.

The body copy

2a. Are all key features expressed as benefits?

Of course, no one buys light bulbs – they buy light. But many ads labour the product features, not what the features will do for the reader.

2b. Is the word 'you' (or its implication) prominent?

'You' is the strongest word in the language. An ad which ignores it, lives dangerously. True, a good ad may never use 'you'. It may be a third-party report or consist of an arresting dialogue between two people, which the reader 'overhears'. But still the reader's presence is implicit. A lot of ads talk only to themselves.

2c. Have you focussed on one main offer?

Should you put several offers in one ad? Yes and no. Offering both a costly, and a less costly but comparable, item in the same ad is risky: readers play safe and go for the cheapie. Of course, this may be what you want: the ad pays for itself on the cheaper products and really makes money from the few customers who buy the luxury version.

One Guild delegate always lists one product in his ad at a very high price, alongside the one he really wants to sell, to stress the value of the cheaper option and the fact that he sells quality. If people buy the more costly one, he wins both ways.

Or you may wish existing customers for the low-cost item to upgrade to the costlier product: then you've sold them twice. Some product ads may be literally a catalogue of different offers and prices. *Yet all these will benefit, if one main offer is highlighted. It flags the reader's eye.*

2d. Are all your claims substantiated in specific terms?

Vague statements like 'many satisfied customers' only convince if rephrased '6753 people to date have tested the flidget' or even '99.5 per cent of customers to date said the flidget satisfactorily solved their problem'. (What about the remaining 0.5 per cent? 'They had, it turned out, a completely different problem. We're working on it! Meanwhile, we returned their money without question'.) Cite numbers, per cents, independent proof – lab tests and Institute reports, named customers and testimonials. Always be *specific*.

2e. Is price omitted or expressed as a benefit?

'Price' and its industrial equivalent 'cost' are negatives. Show them (if you must) as positives: 'For a weekly investment of just £32.50, you gain immediately these six benefits . . .' At least, put the price after the benefits. Often it should not appear at all: the purpose of the ad may be to bring enquiries, so the rep can negotiate price later. Announcing price in your headline without a qualifier can kill. 'Tomorrow's pallet truck today! £1250.' (This – an actual example – might have worked, if the price benefit was obvious: for example, instead of £1250, '. . . for just £50 deposit.')

2f. Does your body copy contain subheads?

Long copy should be broken by subheads, because they provide 'flags' guiding the eye and making it easier to read.

2g. Do subheads convey benefits?

Because most people read the subheads *before* the body copy, they are excellent places to repeat benefits.

2h. Have you targeted the reader?

'Calling Luton men with chilblains!' may be an extreme example, but it pays to make it clear very quickly *who* you are addressing. 'Your field engineers can gain up to 100 per cent faster turnround on parts . . .' disqualifies all readers who lack field engineers. Fine. They weren't going to buy from you anyway. But it tells the rest 'this offer is designed just for you.'

2i. Do you reassure readers that you are a reputable (or credible) supplier?

'Proof statements' like case studies, endorsements and the like obviously help. But can you also cite your memberships of professional institutions, your long track record, numbers or quality of customers, even a guarantee? This can be vital for the most reputable of advertisers. A building society may have no problems with its reputation, but its credibility will be suspect if, say, it suddenly offers a 'direct mail consultancy service'. Unless it can remind us of its long successful experience in the database marketing of financial products . . . and prove it.

2j. Is the copy easy to read?

Even graduates and technicians prefer to read material which is simple and direct, couched in short words, short sentences, and short paragraphs. The longer and more convoluted the 'meaning units', the harder an idea is to understand, and the more readers you lose. Obvious, and yet . . .

2k. Does the copy appeal to emotion as well as logic?

'Picture . . .', 'imagine . . .', 'enjoy . . .', 'achieve . . .', and emotive words like them appeal to the emotion-driven right brain, where buying decisions are often made. (The logical left brain then finds reasons to justify them!) A powerful ad will balance emotional appeals with logical statements; even if selling the most technical of items. Buyers are human.

The call to action

3a. Is there a strong call to action?

Many ads tail off with no indication as to what the readers should do. Return the coupon? Phone a Hotline number? Call a local dealer? Add you to their tender list? Or choose your brand next time they go shopping? 'Corporate' ads are notorious offenders, coyly (and unconvincingly) concealing their intentions. Presumably, they want readers to change their attitudes to the advertiser. But what should readers do now, that they didn't do before? Specify it and you might get it!

3b. Have you motivated the reader to respond now?

What will they gain by acting now (not next month)? A special gift, premium, incentive? What could they lose through delay?

3c. Have you built in 'facilitators'?

They can order by credit card, your telephone lines are open 24 hours (at least, via answering machine), you don't want a cheque up-front – you'll invoice them, they can receive the goods on approval and pay later, they can respond without cost by Freephone or LinkLine or Freepost . . .

3d. Is it clear what will happen when they respond?
'You will receive confirmation of your order by return' . . . 'Your information pack will be sent same day' . . . 'No rep will call' . . . 'Your local dealer will contact you to arrange a no-obligation demonstration' . . .

3e. Can they respond in more than one way?
The more chances you give them to respond, the more responses you'll get. Try a coupon plus a Hotline telephone number plus a Freepost address plus a 'bingo' card number (plus, even, an extra reply card 'tipped on' or stuck over the coupon). These extra devices can cost more, but often repay their investment.

3f. Does the 'call to action' summarise the benefits?
This is your strongest place to sell, after the picture and headline. 'Order now . . .' is not as strong as 'Order now, and remember, you get all these benefits at once . . .' (and the benefits are listed).

3g. Is the coupon easy to complete and/or cut?
Not every ad should have a coupon, but if yours does, can readers use it? It can be worse than useless if space limitations squeeze it to a postage stamp, or – resisting scissors – it bleeds into the magazine spine or (incredible but sometimes true) floats in the *middle* of the ad! Bottom right hand corner is best or, if you don't know which side the magazine will run it, across the entire bottom of the ad.

3h. Is the response device keyed?
How else will you know where the response came from? Or how to change your ad schedule to a more profitable one next time? (Every ad can do this, even

those which *don't* want an instant response. Otherwise, how can you tell if anyone's read the ad – or which is the most productive place for it to appear?)

Ad visuals

4a. Is there a visual element in the ad?

'All copy' ads can work astoundingly well, if they imitate an editorial layout. But all but the smallest editorial-style ads will still pull better, if they contain a photo or illustration. *Because the main picture is where the eye goes first.* Likewise, vary the ad's texture with graphics – flow charts, tables, panels, 'callouts' (an editorial device, these are quotes extracted from your text and set in a panel).

4b. Is the main picture large enough?

Having stopped the eye, give it something substantial to see.

4c. Is the picture of good quality?

Newspaper and directory ads in particular reproduce photos poorly. These, and line illustrations which are not professionally done, can kill your credibility.

4d. Does the picture show more than just the product?

'Pack shots' may have a place in editorial product reviews, but they are dreadfully boring used as the key element of an ad.

4e. Does the picture demonstrate benefits?

A picture which serves merely to 'stop the eye' is like a cute headline which screams 'Free money! (Now that I have your interest, let's discuss my product . . .).' Readers feel cheated. And nowadays, irrelevantly glamorous model girls insult them. Stop the eye, by all means, but with a dramatically illustrated *benefit*.

4f.   Is the picture a cliché?

Dinosaurs, ostriches with their heads in the sand, businessmen with question marks on their forehead (or wilting beside over-full in-trays or wearing blindfolds), happy hurdlers leaping for the winning line, 'breakthroughs' dramatised by collapsing walls (or 'holes' bursting through the page) . . . all are the signs of a tired designer. Surely *your* benefit is more original?

4g.   Are people shown enjoying the benefits?

It helps to put the reader 'in the picture' if you do just that. To reach mothers, show babies. To impress works managers, show credible employees using your product . . .

4h.   Is the picture captioned?

If the picture goes at the top of the ad, the headline itself can serve as a caption. Otherwise, you need a caption. It's where readers look, after seeing the picture and glancing at the headline.

4i.   Does the caption convey a benefit?

Don't waste this 'hot' space with a mere description. Reinforce the benefit shown in the picture.

4j.   Is the path for the reader's eye clearly flagged?

Readers in Western countries learn to read from top to bottom, left to right. Don't confuse them by putting major design elements (picture, headline, tinted panels, coupon, and the like) in an illogical order. The eye gives up. Particularly, *don't* play games with the reader by reversing an ad, or running it sideways, or having different elements at right angles. Reader's won't play.

4k.   Is the layout *too* balanced?

Brochure designers delight in 'squaring up' a layout so nicely it has all the dynamic tension of a mortuary slab. A calculated imperfection – a picture or panel, say, at a slant – pulls more response. (It's one reason why catalogue mailers print the reply card as a hang-down flap. Readers would be less likely to spoil the mailer's symmetry by cutting a coupon, but they'll tear off that irritating flap.)

4l.   Has the 'call to action' been emphasised with a graphic element?

A panel, or second colour, or flash guides the reader to the action point.

4m.   Is the headline visually strong?

It can be a mistake to run a long headline entirely in capitals. Caps are far harder to read than lower case. And a headline should not be dominated by other design elements to the point where a busy reader might miss it completely.

4n.   Do you really want your company logo that big?

Unless the entire point of your ad is to say 'Watch for this sign . . . it's a symbol of (quality)'. Logos alone rarely convey benefits.

4o.   Have you used a readable typeface?

Serif type is the kind with the little tails. Sans serif has no tails. Editors know well that serif type (e.g. *Times*) is far more readable in body copy than sans serif type (e.g. Helvetica). Ad designers do not know this. Or else they would not persist in using sans serif in ten points or smaller, which is virtually impossible to read.

4p. Have you avoided using white out of black for body copy?

This is powerful as a headline, but does not work well in body copy. Likewise, avoid laying small text over heavy tints or second colours.

4q. Do tints or spot colours (where used) emphasise copy elements?

Or are they just there to make your ad look nice? Avoid the latter! The only beautiful ad is the one that works.

If you can say *yes* to all these questions, yours is an ad that should pull and pull. Provided, of course, it is read by the right people. And it sells something worth buying. This book tries to help with the former. But alas, with the latter, you're on your own. Good luck!

BIBLIOGRAPHY

Considine, Ray and Raphel, Murray, *The Great Brain Robbery*, via Hoke Communications, 224 7th Street, Garden City, New York 11530, 1981.

Crompton, Alastair, *The Craft of Copywriting*, Business Books, 1979.

Crompton, Alastair, *Do Your Own Advertising*, Gold Farthing Press, 1985.

Graham, John W. and Jones, Susan K., *Selling by Mail*, Charles Scribners Sons, New York, 1985.

Holtz, Herman, *The Direct Marketers Workbook*, John Wiley and Sons, New York, 1986.

Korda, Michael, *Success*, Ballantine.

Levinson, Jay Conrad, *Guerilla Marketing*, Houghton Mifflin Co., Boston, 1984.

Lewis, Herschell Gordon, *How to Make Your Advertising Twice as Effective at Half the Cost*, Prentice Hall Inc., 1986.

Lumley, James E. A., *Sell it by Mail*, John Wiley & Sons, 1986.

Ogilvy, David, *Confessions of an Advertising Man*, Atheneum, New York, 1962.

Ogilvy, David, *Ogilvy on Advertising*, Guild Publishing (with Pan Books), London, 1985.

Post Office, *The Direct Mail Handbook*, 1984.

Rapp, Stan and Collins, Tom, *MaxiMarketing*, McGraw-Hill, 1987.

Rein, Irving, *High Visibility*, Heinemann.

Ries, Al and Trout, Jack, *Positioning: The Battle for Your Mind*, Warner Books, 1981.

Schmertz, H., *Goodbye to the Low Profile*, Mercury Business Books, W. H. Allen & Co. Plc.

Smith, Cynthia S., *How to Get Big Results From a Small Advertising Budget*, Hawthorn Books, New York, 1973.

Weintz, Walter H., *The Solid Gold Mail Box*, John Wiley & Sons, 1987.

For an information pack about Marketing Guild membership, contact: The Marketing Guild Ltd, FREEPOST LOL 2052, Unit 1, Houghton Court, Houghton Regis, Beds LU5 5DY (0582–861556)

Also by Nick Robinson

PERSUASIVE BUSINESS PRESENTATIONS

This practical handbook contains hundreds of tested ideas to help you persuade people through the spoken word – more powerfully and profitably. All are based on Nick Robinson's 20 years' experience of selling effectively through personal presentations. He used the knowledge revealed in this book to build the Datanews group, one of Britain's most successful marketing and PR consultancies.

Nick Robinson's advice works, whether you are selling 'big ticket' products or services before powerful buying groups, or addressing your sales conference, or leading a staff meeting, or simply presenting your case to your employer or an individual customer. You can apply his step-by-step plans to enhance your career – or make your business grow – now.

£12.95 in hardback   **ISBN 1 85251 053 6**